UNBELIEVABLE!

The Bizarre World of
Coincidences

JENNY CROMPTON

Michael O'Mara Books Limited

First published in Great Britain in 2013 by
Michael O'Mara Books Limited
9 Lion Yard
Tremadoc Road
London SW4 7NQ

A CIP catalogue record for this book is available from the British
Library.

Papers used by Michael O'Mara Books Limited are natural,
recyclable products made from wood grown in sustainable forests.
The manufacturing processes conform to the environmental
regulations of the country of origin.

ISBN: 978-1-78243-038-4 in hardback print format
ISBN: 978-1-78243-089-6 in ePub format
ISBN: 978-1-78243-090-2 in Mobipocket format

1 2 3 4 5 6 7 8 9 10

Printed and bound by CPI Group (UK) Ltd, Croydon, CR0 4YY

www.mombooks.com

Illustrations by Greg Stevenson
Jacket design by David Sinden
Designed and typeset by K DESIGN, Somerset

CONTENTS

INTRODUCTION

'No coincidence, no story.'

CHINESE SAYING

COINCIDENCES make the best stories.

Listen carefully next time you're at a dinner party and you'll notice how many anecdotes start 'I've had the most ridiculously unlucky day' or 'You'll never believe who we ran into at that dodgy motel' or 'Did you know Hitler almost became an artist rather than a psychopath?' – to be met by a chorus of 'What are the odds?' and 'How weird!' and everybody trying to outdo each other with ever more improbable yarns. Skimming just the top of my own greatest hits: I've bumped into an old school friend in the Australian Outback, checked into the wrong hotel room because the rightful occupant shared my name, discovered in the course of casual chitchat that my boss was the son of my university professor, and narrowly avoided being involved in a terrorist incident because I was horribly hung over and late for work. (The latter arguably less of a coincidence than a lifestyle choice.) Coincidences are all around us, if only we can find the link that transforms two unrelated – and often uninteresting – circumstances into an incredible tale.

Depending on your disposition and your level of involvement in the story, coincidence has any number of alter egos: irony, conspiracy, karma, fate, destiny, good or bad luck, premonition, divine intervention, or just plain old Sod's Law. Via lottery wins, lucky guesses and survival against the odds, coincidence has a hand in everything from the unlikely victory of 'Harry, England and Saint George' in Shakespeare's *Henry V* to poor old Alanis Morissette's unexpected windfall of 10,000 spoons when the one thing she needs is a sodding knife.

But are coincidences just tenuous man-made connections or is there anything more profound at work? Without doubt we love to *interpret* them as meaningful rather than random: ask people who consider themselves lucky and you'll find their own strings of happy coincidences are a sign that 'someone's watching out for me'; less fortunate people, on the other hand, will likely seize on every new misadventure as yet further proof that they are nothing but the playthings of cruel Fate.

The philosopher and psychologist Carl Jung certainly thought there was something to it all, developing in the early 1950s his theory of synchronicity: 'the simultaneous occurrence of events that appear significantly related but have no discernible causal connection', or, in plain English, the grouping together of events by meaning rather than by cause (see p.23 for one of his own examples). Jung's studies on the matter veer into the overly technical for our purposes here, but on a day-to-day level we all experience these seemingly meaningful coincidences: thinking about someone just as they inexplicably round the corner, reading a word in a book at the same moment it appears in the lyrics of a song on the radio, idly daydreaming about spending imaginary millions just seconds before discovering we're the sole inheritor of a mystery great-aunt's vast estate ... The most cynical of people would be hard pressed not to think 'It must be a sign'.

Of course, seeking the hidden meaning behind every coincidence is what leads us into the realms of curses and conspiracy theories, or the near-universal fear of the number 13. Nary a major world event, from a celebrity death to an election win, can go by these days without a sizeable faction pointing to seemingly incidental circumstances as proof of a secret plot. (By the way, did you know Michael Jackson was buried on the anniversary of his will being signed? Did you know most United States presidents are left-handed? Mighty strange, that's all I'm saying ...)

Coincidences are, above all, cracking stories, and alongside the spooky, scary and downright suspicious, this book celebrates the bizarre and funny ones, too: long-lost lovers, godsends that quite literally fall from the heavens, and the weird and wonderful workings of the cosmic lost-property cupboard. Hundreds of tales from all over the world that are so unbelievable they *must* be true.

'The most astonishingly incredible
coincidence imaginable would
be the complete absence of all
coincidences.'

JOHN ALLEN PAULOS

A STROKE OF LUCK

THE best coincidences are those that end happily: saved lives, lottery wins, chance encounters and inadvertent brainwaves. From finding yourself in the right place at the right time to realizing you've had a fortunate escape, the lighter side of luck is a joy to behold.

> 'Twenty-four hours in a day; twenty-four beers in a case. Coincidence?'
> STEVEN WRIGHT

CHEATING DEATH

While some people seem to court calamity – as the next chapter amply proves – others seem simply to toy with it before making a lucky escape. Again and again and again …

⇒⇒●⇐⇐

NINE LIVES, PLUS FIVE

Pensioner Alec Alder was dubbed 'Britain's luckiest man' after it was revealed that he had cheated death not once but fourteen times.

Alder's first encounter with the Grim Reaper was at the age of seven, when he fell out of a fifteen-foot tree. Three years later, aged ten, he was hit by a car while out cycling. The head-on collision sent him flying into the air and onto the bonnet, but as luck would have it the driver was a doctor and was able to give him immediate medical assistance.

At the outbreak of World War II, Alder was due to be shipped off to France but was given a few days' leave to get married, after which he was sent on a different mission on home soil.

'My old company went off to Dunkirk,' he later recalled. 'All my friends got killed and I should have been with them.'

The war was not to be entirely uneventful for him, though. He was bombed twice in 1940, and in 1942 he was run over by a tank during training; thanks to heavy rain it merely pushed his foot and leg into the mud before miraculously stalling inches from his head. That same year, a British fighter plane crash-landed on the Devon house in which Alder was visiting relatives, bursting into flame and causing the roof to collapse into his bedroom.

Having somehow reached the end of the war alive, despite further near-death encounters on the high seas and in Burma, his ship home almost sank in a terrible storm off the coast of Gibraltar. He made it back to Britain, where he subsequently survived three horrifying near-misses in his car before dying of natural causes at the ripe old age of eighty-eight.

TWISTER TROUBLE

In Songjiang, China, in 1992, locals watched in horror as a freak whirlwind swept up a nine-year-old girl and carried her away. After an exhaustive search, she was found dazed but unharmed in a tree two miles away from where she had been playing. Incredibly, the same thing had happened six years earlier in the west of China when thirteen children were swept twelve miles by a sudden gust but dropped unhurt onto sand dunes.

Your Number's Up

When Melbourne truck driver Bill Morgan died from a massive heart attack in 1998, he was in fact on the cusp of an incredible string of luck.

Fourteen minutes after being pronounced dead, Morgan came back to life – only to fall into a coma from which doctors were convinced he would never wake. Twelve days later, however, he did just that, much to the delight of his family, who had been advised to switch off his life-support machine.

With his new-found sense of mortality, Morgan threw himself into all that life had to offer. He began dating Lisa Wells and proposed to her on the anniversary of his death. She accepted. Sensing that his luck might be in, he bought a lottery scratch card and sure enough won a car worth A$17,000.

All of this would have been remarkable enough but the best was yet to come. A TV crew came to film a short piece on Morgan's incredible good fortune and asked him to re-enact his scratch card win. With the camera rolling, he casually scratched the ticket and then stared at it in disbelief before bursting into tears: he had won another A$250,000.

Perhaps more convinced than ever that she had chosen the right man, Ms Wells commented: 'I just hope he hasn't used all his good luck up.'

Mr Calamity

Ever the optimist, one of the world's unluckiest men considers himself the luckiest thanks to his uncanny knack for cheating death. In 2006 it was revealed that Doncaster grandfather John Lyne had notched up sixteen incredible near-misses in his fifty-four years.

But Mr Lyne's death-dodging life almost ended on day one, when he was born with underdeveloped lungs and needed round-the-clock care. Having survived that, he next visited casualty aged just eighteen months after downing a bottle of disinfectant he had found in his grandmother's bathroom. As a toddler he was almost run over by a van but was fortunately small enough to fall between its wheels rather than under them.

After a decade's welcome respite, Mr Lyne's rate of calamities went into overdrive during his teens, when he was struck by lightning, hit in the face by a catapult-propelled rock, and almost drowned. On one inauspicious Friday 13th, he broke his arm falling out of a tree. The next day he and his mother were involved in a road accident in which he broke another bone in the same arm.

Mr Lyne tempted fate by choosing a career in the mines, and fate did not disappoint: on one occasion he narrowly avoided being crushed by falling rock. He was subsequently electrocuted in a DIY mishap, almost killed on holiday – twice – and badly injured in several places after falling down a manhole.

'With all the bumps and scrapes over the years I have been very lucky,' he told the *Daily Mail*. 'I should be winning the lottery next.'

———⟫●⟪———

WHAT ARE THE ODDS?

These extraordinary tales of synchronicity make your everyday experiences of coincidence pale into insignificance.

———⟫●⟪———

DODGY DECK

Bucklesham Whist Club in Suffolk enjoyed its fifteen minutes of fame in January 1998 when a seemingly innocent game of cards between three OAPs defied

2,235,197,406,895,366,368,301,599,999-to-one odds.

In an intrigue worthy of Miss Marple, eighty-seven-year-old Hilda Golding looked at her cards to find she had been dealt all thirteen clubs. She glanced over at her opponents and saw the same look of astonishment on their faces: one of them had all the diamonds, one had all the hearts, and the 'dummy' player had all the spades. Suspicion immediately fell upon the shuffler, Alison Chivers, who had prepared the hall before the Whist Club's arrival and who subsequently

won the hand thanks to hearts being trumps, but it quickly transpired that this particular deck had been shuffled by the third player before the game started – and there were fifty-five witnesses to prove it.

———➤●◄———

'I busted a mirror and got seven years' bad luck, but my lawyer thinks he can get me five.'

STEVEN WRIGHT

———➤●◄———

POLE POSITION

The 1997 European Grand Prix is probably best known among Formula One fans as the meeting at which the Williams and McLaren teams were accused of race-fixing. The more interesting story, however, happened before the race had even begun.

During qualifying, each driver was given an hour to make up to twelve timed laps of the course, his fastest time being used to decide grid position for the main event. After fourteen minutes, Jacques Villeneuve achieved what turned out to be his best speed – one minute and 21.072 seconds – which was followed another fourteen minutes later by Michael Schumacher recording the exact same time. Incredibly, just minutes later, Heinz-Harald Frentzen made his own fastest circuit: one minute and 21.072 seconds. By an incredible – and unprecedented – fluke, three drivers were in pole position.

Not that it helped any of them to glory that day. Having started the race at 1, 2 and 3, in the order in which they achieved the qualifying time, Villeneuve scraped third position after a collision with Schumacher, which forced the latter to bow out, while Frentzen came sixth.

<hr />

Waking Dream

The analytical psychologist Carl Jung used the word synchronicity to describe what, in technical jargon, he called 'temporarily coincident occurrences of acausal events', or 'a strange coincidence' to you and me.

Jung's favourite example of synchronicity, which he related in his book of the same name, occurred during a session with one of his clients:

'A young woman I was treating had, at a critical moment, a dream in which she was given a golden scarab. While she was telling me this dream I sat with my back to the closed window. Suddenly I heard a noise behind me, like a gentle tapping. I turned round and saw a flying insect knocking against the window-pane from outside. I opened the window and caught the creature in the air as it flew in. It was the nearest analogy to the golden scarab that one finds in our latitudes, a scarabaeid beetle, the common rose-chafer, which contrary to its usual habits had evidently felt an urge to get into a dark room at this particular moment.'

A Dessert with Destiny

In his memoirs, the nineteenth-century French poet Emile Deschamps tells of how, as a boy, he was introduced to plum pudding by an acquaintance named Monsieur de **Fortgibu**. The unremarkable incident was all but forgotten until, ten years later, Deschamps saw plum pudding on a restaurant menu and remembered having enjoyed it. Alas, the waiter informed him, the last piece of plum pudding had just been ordered by the gentleman in the corner – who turned out to be M. de Fortgibu.

A number of years later, Deschamps, now in his forties, was at a dinner party and learned that the dessert was plum pudding. He regaled the assembled company with his unusual experiences with the dessert and joked that the only thing missing this evening was M. de Fortgibu. Just at that moment, the door swung open and in walked that very gentleman.

In his senility, he had wandered through the wrong door by mistake.

'Three times in my life I have eaten plum pudding, and three times I have seen Monsieur de Fortgibu,' Deschamps exclaimed. 'My hair stood on end!'

GOOD TIMING

Fate often seems to put us in the right place at the right time – quite remarkable when you consider how every tiny decision or hesitation sends you, *Sliding Doors*-style, towards a new destiny. The following stories are about apparent disasters that turn out to be cases of excellent timing.

AFFAIRS OF THE HEART

As Dorothy Fletcher of Liverpool knows only too well, there are few worse places to have a heart attack than on a transatlantic flight – unless fifteen of your fellow passengers are cardiologists on their way to a conference.

Mrs Fletcher was flying from Manchester to Florida for her daughter's wedding in November 2003 when disaster struck. The stewards put out an urgent appeal for any doctors on board to make themselves known.

'I couldn't believe what happened,' Mrs Fletcher later recalled. 'All these people came rushing down the aircraft towards me.'

The cardiologists were able to keep her stable while the plane was diverted to North Carolina, and she even made it to the wedding as planned.

Lucky Lateness

Many incredible stories of survival emerged in the aftermath of 9/11, but one that remained strangely unreported was that of diminutive kung fu star Jackie Chan narrowly avoiding being atop the World Trade Center on the morning of the attack.

According to the Singapore newspaper *Straits Times*, Chan had been due to start filming *Nosebleed* at 7 a.m. on 11 September 2001 – specifically a scene in which he, a World Trade Center window cleaner, sees and falls in love with a waitress working at the Windows on the World restaurant at the top of the North Tower. But because there was a delay in getting him the script for this scene, Chan travelled to Canada instead to do some work on another film. *Nosebleed* was ultimately cancelled.

'I would probably have died if the shooting went ahead as planned,' Chan is reported to have said. 'I guess my time is not up yet.'

Buckle Up

In April 2013 a supermarket employee in Philadelphia, Pennsylvania was saved from certain death, if not by the skin of his teeth then by the buckle of his belt.

Bienvenido Reynoso was standing near the door when he heard shots and dropped to the ground. All around him bullets were hitting the shelves and windows; food and glass were flying everywhere but Reynoso himself was mercifully not shot at.

Or so he thought. A little later he noticed something lodged in his belt buckle, which upon closer inspection turned out to be a stray bullet.

'I am reborn today,' a relieved Reynoso told reporters.

EUREKA!

When Isaac Newton sat down under a tree one day to contemplate the universe, only to be struck on the head by a falling apple and suddenly notice that gravity existed, it was less of a one-off miracle than the start of the most glorious tradition in modern-day science: unintentional genius. (In fact, Newton himself was following in the noble footsteps of Archimedes, who suffered an accidental revelation about density and volume while enjoying a relaxing bath and was so overjoyed that he ran through the streets naked.)

MOULD MAGIC

Proving that tedious housework is always best put off for another day, a sink full of bacteria-ridden lab equipment is credited with literally having spawned one of the most important medicines in human history.

Alexander Fleming locked up his London lab one evening in September 1928 without bothering to do the dishes. When he returned a few days later and reluctantly began to tackle the toxic detritus of his failed experiments, he noticed that one Petri dish containing a staphylococcus culture had begun to grow blue mould, and that the mould had apparently killed any staphylococcus bacteria it had come into contact with.

Fleming conducted a series of experiments on this miraculous mould – presumably leaving his washing up to its own scientific endeavours – and determined that it was *Penicillium notatum*, now more commonly known as penicillin.

———≫●≪———

'What separates the winners from
the losers is how a person reacts to
each new twist of fate.'

DONALD TRUMP

———›❂‹———

ADVENTURES IN ALGEBRA

In 1995, after nine years of intense number-crunching, Oxford professor John Wiles solved Fermat's Last Theorem, a calculation so complex that generations of mathematicians before him had gone to their graves still trying to complete it. He won a host of international prizes and was knighted for his efforts. But all Wiles had actually managed to do was, in true maths-teacher style, 'show the workings' of a lazier mathematician who had somehow solved the problem an incredible 358 years earlier.

When, in 1637, Pierre de Fermat scribbled a note in the margin of his copy of Diophantus' *Arithmetica*, he could hardly have known the centuries of mathematical chaos he was about to unleash. For all anyone knows he may even have been joking when he jotted down a contentious new theory and stated:

'I have discovered a truly marvellous proof of this, which this margin is too narrow to contain' – but the undisputable fact is that he was spot on.

Given that even Sir John Wiles' proof of this used maths Fermat could not possibly have known and yet still contained gaps, we have to wonder: was Fermat's Last Theorem, the world's most difficult maths problem, just an incredibly lucky guess?

———⟫●⟪———

Hot Chocolate

Towards the end of World War II, an American engineer named Percy Spencer was working for a company developing new radar technology designed for use in combat. As he fired off some radar beams as part of an experiment, he suddenly realized the Hershey's chocolate bar in his pocket was steadily turning to mulch. Upon closer inspection he made an incredible discovery: the rays were cooking the chocolate.

In the lab, Spencer cobbled together a metal box in which he zapped various food items, popping corn and exploding eggs to the great amazement of his

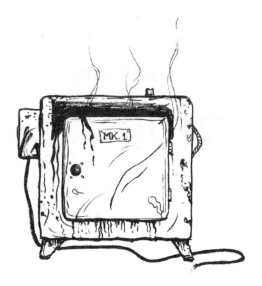

colleagues. It was only a matter of time before his employers snapped up the patent to the first microwave oven, which they marketed as the Radarange: a six-foot, 750-pound contraption that cost the equivalent of $50,000.

HOW
UNFORTUNATE

FOR every lucky person out there, it seems fate has decreed someone else must be less fortunate. As Franklin D. Roosevelt very wisely pointed out, 'I think we consider too much the good luck of the early bird and not enough the bad luck of the early worm.' Life's early worms are those who appear destined to be in the wrong place at the wrong time – often repeatedly – as these sorry tales attest.

'Destiny is a good thing to accept
when it's going your way. When
it isn't, don't call it destiny; call it
injustice, treachery, or simple bad
luck.'

JOSEPH HELLER

———>●<———

A SERIES OF UNFORTUNATE EVENTS

The people involved in these strings of calamitous coincidences might well have asked what on earth they had done to deserve it. Whether they were cursed from birth or simply got out of bed on the wrong side, one thing is clear: they're all out of luck.

———>●<———

UNLUCKY STRIKE

In 2010 the National Weather Service in the United States estimated that the likelihood of an American citizen being struck by lightning once in an eighty-year lifetime was 1:10,000. What they made of Roy Sullivan, who in a thirty-four-year period was struck by lightning a Guinness World Record-holding seven times, is not known.

Sullivan, a park ranger at Virginia's Shenandoah National Park, suffered his first strike in 1942 while hiding from a storm in a building with no lightning conductor. In 1969 he was struck in highly improbable circumstances: the lightning bounced off a tree and into his open car window. The following year he

was struck in his garden and in 1972 while once again sheltering inside a building. By now Sullivan had become so paranoid that he took to running away from approaching storm clouds – to no avail in both 1973 and 1976. In 1977 he was unwinding with a spot of fishing when lightning struck his head; unbelievably, as he crawled back to his car, he had to fight off a bear that was trying to steal his fish.

CATCH A FALLING STAR

In all of human history, only one person is unlucky enough to have been struck by a falling meteorite. And while the laws of probability dictate that meteorites will generally fall into uninhabited areas such as deserts or oceans, this one landed on a woman who was snoozing on her sofa at home.

In November 1954, Ann Hodges was asleep in her lounge in Sylacauga, Alabama, when a chunk of space rock crashed through her ceiling and hit her, causing an enormous bruise on her thigh but leaving her otherwise unharmed.

'You have a better chance of getting hit by a tornado and a bolt of lightning and a hurricane all at the same time,' astronomer Michael Reynolds told *National Geographic*.

━━━➤●◄━━━

FOR THE CHOP

The invention of the guillotine was attributed to and named after Dr Joseph-Ignace Guillotin, an eighteenth-century French physician who was opposed to the death penalty but did propose the use of a device to carry out executions for humane reasons. The actual inventor of the guillotine prototype was one Antoine Louis. The Guillotin family were unsuccessful in petitioning the French government to change the name of the device, so resorted to changing their own name instead. By coincidence a doctor from Lyon named Guillotin was guillotined during those brutal revolutionary years in France – a coincidence that led many to assume that he and the inventor were one and the same. The original Monsieur Guillotin, however, died in Paris in 1814 of natural causes.

TICKET TO HELL

Choosing a holiday destination became the stuff of nightmares for Birmingham couple Jason and Jenny Cairns-Lawrence after they inexplicably witnessed three international terrorist atrocities over seven years.

The Cairns-Lawrences were visiting New York in September 2001 when the Twin Towers were struck by planes; they were in London for a few days in July 2005 when three tube trains and a bus were bombed; and they were in Mumbai in November 2008 when a coordinated shooting and bombing spree brought tragedy to the city.

In something of an understatement, Mrs Cairns-Lawrence told reporters: 'It's a strange coincidence. The terror attacks just happened when we were in the cities.'

UNHAPPY VALENTINE

Valentine's Day in 1884 was a date to remember for future president Theodore Roosevelt, but tragically for all the wrong reasons.

Just hours after the death of his beloved mother, Roosevelt lost his young wife, Alice, in childbirth. It was the fourth anniversary of their engagement.

TR's diary entry for that day simply reads: 'X. The light has gone out of my life.'

STRANGER THAN FICTION

Jeanne Rogers of Bangor, Maine has led the kind of life that would look unrealistic in even the most farcical of slapstick comedies.

In 1967, Rogers and a friend were on a cruise and chose the moment just after a heavy downpour to take photos of each other on deck. In a textbook case of 'Back a bit … Back a bit further …', Rogers fell overboard and her friend then knocked herself out trying to summon help. The massive liner was eventually turned around. In 1971 she was struck by lightning, which blew off her shoes and melted her tights, and two years later she was struck by lightning again.

Family life did not prove much of a respite. One day, while out with her son, a bat nosedived her and sunk its claws into her scalp. In panic she ran from house to house screaming for help but was met with horrified faces and slammed doors. This served only to panic the bat, which dug in deeper and urinated on her head. Rogers was forced to drive herself to the vet with the bat still attached ('I drove like a bat out of hell,' she quipped to the *Bangor Daily News*), and subsequently had to wear a beret for three months while her hair grew back.

She has also survived being mugged, shot at while horse riding, and strangled by her drunken husband.

'Dying doesn't scare me,' she told the paper in 2007, 'but living scares the crap out of me.'

―――――>●<―――――

HMS CALAMITY

Violet Jessop chose a career in nursing to help those in distress, but during her years of service aboard various ocean liners she quickly became notorious as an angel of doom.

In 1911, Violet took a job on the RMS *Olympic*, the largest passenger liner of its day, and soon witnessed a near-disastrous collision with another ship off the coast of the Isle of Wight. The following year she joined the crew of the *Olympic*'s sister ship, the RMS *Titanic*, whose tragic tale is legendary. Fortunate enough to make it into one of the lifeboats, Violet returned to England in time for the outbreak of World War I, during which she worked for the Red Cross aboard the third ship in the Olympic-class trio: HMHS *Britannic*. In 1916 the ship hit a mine and sank in the Aegean.

Despite hitting her head on the ship's keel as she leapt overboard, Violet survived her third marine disaster. More unbelievable still, she didn't call time on her ocean-going career until 1950.

———⇒●⇐———

Dad: 'The world isn't fair, Calvin.'
Calvin: 'I know, but why isn't it ever unfair in my favor?'

BILL WATTERSON, *CALVIN AND HOBBES*

———⇒●⇐———

TERRIBLE TIMING

As every actor knows, timing is everything. Get it right and the world smiles upon you; get it wrong and ... well, you'll see.

———⟫●⟪———

Method Acting

Brad Pitt went all out to get into character on the set of *Troy* (2004), but it was probably a performance he'd rather forget than win an Oscar for.

During a particularly tricky fight scene against his enemy, Hector, Pitt leapt and landed badly, tearing his Achilles tendon in the process and ruling out the filming of other fight scenes for a number of weeks. Apt, considering Pitt was portraying Achilles, the mythical Greek hero whose heel was his only, er, Achilles heel.

———⟫●⟪———

Deutsch Dilemma

In the years since World War II there has been approximately one case a year of Foreign Accent Syndrome, when a person – often following a head injury – awakes with a speech impediment that strongly resembles a foreign accent. But by far the most unfortunate case occurred during the war itself, when a woman from Norway, which was under Nazi occupation at the time, came to after a shrapnel attack with a strong German accent. She was all but chased out of her village.

———⟫●⟪———

Nuclear Nightmare

In the summer of 1945, Mitsubishi draughtsman Tsutomu Yamaguchi was dispatched by his employers to Hiroshima on a three-month assignment. On the morning of his last day he was walking to work at the shipyard when he noticed a military plane in the sky.

'I looked up into the sky and saw the B-29, and it dropped two parachutes,' he told reporters many years later. 'I was looking up at them, and suddenly it was like a flash of magnesium, a great flash in the sky, and I was blown over.'

The date was 6 August 1945 and Yamaguchi had been knocked down by the force of an atomic bomb. Although he was some kilometres away from the blast, he still suffered burns to his chest.

After two nights in an air-raid shelter, Yamaguchi felt the coast was clear and returned home to Nagasaki. The following day, 9 August, he reported for work as usual. During a debriefing with his boss, 'the whole office, everything in it, was blown over.' It was the second – and final – atomic bomb attack on Japan.

Incredibly Yamaguchi survived once again, this time unscathed. Although it is thought that others were equally unlucky in witnessing both nuclear attacks, he is to date the only officially recognized 'double-survivor'. He died aged 93 in 2010.

'Fortune brings in some boats that are not steer'd.'

SHAKESPEARE, *CYMBELINE*

Posthumous Praise

In 1963, twenty-five-year-old John Kennedy Toole, a reclusive New Orleans English teacher who lived with his mother, completed his comic satire *A Confederacy of Dunces*. For six years he submitted, revised and reworked the novel, but it was rejected by publishers time and again. In 1969, at the age of thirty-one, a depressed Toole committed suicide.

The original manuscript has never been found – it may have been destroyed by Toole before his death – but his mother later stumbled upon a 'badly smeared, scarcely readable' carbon copy of the hefty novel among his possessions; she not only read it but made it her mission to get the book published. After encountering similar setbacks to her son, in desperation she asked Walker Percy, an author and lecturer at the local university, for help. He agreed, very reluctantly, to read it, later recalling 'There was no getting out of it; only one hope remained – that I could read a few pages and that they would be bad enough for me, in good conscience, to read no farther ... In this case I read on. And on. First with the sinking feeling that it was not bad enough to quit, then with a prickle of interest, then a growing excitement, and finally an incredulity: surely it was not possible that it was so good.'

In 1980, with the most tragic irony given its author had abandoned all hope eleven years previously, *A Confederacy of Dunces* was finally published by the tiny Louisiana State University Press. In 1981 it won the Pulitzer Prize.

———➤●◄———

IMPOSSIBLE TITLE

Proving that no amount of international fame can counter the weight of public emotion, pop star Kylie Minogue felt compelled to make an expensive and time-consuming last-minute change to the title of her 1997 album following the death of Princess Diana in August of that year. The rather unimaginative new title was *Kylie Minogue*; the original had been *Impossible Princess*.

———➤●◄———

Leaky Logic

One of New Zealand's most prominent bands of the 1970s and 80s found themselves at the centre of a bizarre British propaganda controversy thanks to the outbreak of the Falklands War.

Split Enz, whose members included Neil and Tim Finn, subsequently of the internationally acclaimed Crowded House, released a single in 1982 that reached no. 2 in Australia and no. 7 in New Zealand and Canada. It has been named the fifth best New Zealand song of all time by the Australasian Performing Rights Association. In the UK, it was banned from airplay by the BBC.

Why? Despite being about the arrival of the first pioneers in New Zealand and having a video featuring Maori dancing, the song's title, 'Six Months in a Leaky Boat', was deemed bad for morale during a naval crisis.

A MOMENT OF MADNESS

Have you ever found yourself in a sticky situation and traced it back to a spectacularly bad decision you needn't have made? You are not alone. As these often cringeworthy coincidences show, history is full of really rather bad ideas.

———⋙●⋘———

MAMMA MIA!

Police in Bari, Italy, were able to apprehend a thief who had grabbed a woman's handbag as he sped past on his motorbike, after she gave them an exceptionally detailed description of him. It turned out she was his mother.

———⋙●⋘———

WORLD'S WORST SANDWICH

In a bizarre tale that is 'right place at the right time' for one of the protagonists and very much 'wrong place at the wrong time' for the other, a humble sandwich unwittingly sparked World War I.

Sarajevo, 28 June 1914: as Archduke Franz Ferdinand was driven through the streets to apparent popular jubilation, six young anti-Empire activists lay in wait with grenades. The first bottled out at the last minute; the second threw his grenade but it exploded under the wrong car, wounding both dignitaries and spectators. In the ensuing chaos, the remaining would-be assassins fled and dispersed, their patriotic plot a failure. One of them, Gavrilo Princip, wandered off to get a sandwich.

Once out of danger, the Archduke asked his driver to take him to the hospital where the injured bystanders were being treated. The driver, perhaps operating on autopilot, started along a road that would take them back through the centre of town before realizing his mistake and making an abrupt stop to turn around – right outside the café where Princip was eating his sandwich. As the driver struggled to find reverse gear and ultimately stalled the car, the young nationalist approached the vehicle and shot the Archduke at point-blank range.

The rest, as they say, is history.

Nice Outfit

A burglar brought before a court in Bruges was surprised to have an impromptu new accusation levelled at him before his trial had even begun. He had donned his Sunday best for the court appearance but it soon became apparent that the clothes were in fact somebody else's Sunday best – specifically, the prosecutor's. Marc Florens immediately recognized the jacket that had been stolen from his house months earlier along with cash and other valuables.

Delayed Karma

When Texan Henry Ziegland jilted his girlfriend in 1883 and was shot at in revenge by her brother, he must have counted himself incredibly lucky to have survived. The bullet merely grazed his cheek and embedded itself in a tree. Meanwhile, the would-be assassin had turned the gun on himself.

Years later, the doomed romance all but forgotten, Ziegland was trying in vain to chop down the same tree. Deciding the only thing for it was dynamite, he created an explosion that did the trick, although it also dislodged the bullet, which shot out into his head and killed him.

———⟫●⟪———

A Cunning Plan

Two burglars broke into a house in Austin, Texas in March 1977 while its owners, David Conner and Nancy Hart, were at work. Among other things, they stole the couple's chequebooks. Thinking they'd make a quick profit before the police had time to catch them, they went into a bank to cash one of Mr

Conner's cheques, which they'd cunningly made out to Ms Hart.

Unfortunately for them, the cashier at said bank was in fact Nancy Hart. She made sure they were detained by security until the police arrived.

———✦———

'One likes people much better
when they're battered down by a
prodigious siege of misfortune than
when they triumph.'

VIRGINIA WOOLF, *A WRITER'S DIARY*

Fancy Meeting You Here

Sometimes news of somebody else's stroke of spectacularly bad luck brings with it a guilty little morsel of schadenfreude – as in this story of unfaithfulness uncovered.

In 1994, two Bulgarian couples on holiday by the Black Sea got to talking and quickly became firm friends. So firm, in fact, that the husband of one couple and the wife of the other were soon embroiled in a torrid affair. Swept up in their own illicit romance, the cheaters were blissfully unaware that their other halves had also embarked upon an affair. None of this might ever have emerged had Couple A not escaped for a secret weekend away the following summer, only to find themselves in the cottage next door to Couple B.

According to Bulgarian newspaper *24 Chasa*, the husbands watched helplessly as their wives physically attacked one another, but had to step in when the women began brandishing hoes as makeshift weapons. Lesson learned, each man left with his own wife in tow.

HISTORY REPEATING

A number of historical artefacts seem destined to reappear time and time again – flares and their nemesis skinny jeans, records, fondue, horn-rimmed specs – but replicated events are far more rare. Not impossible, though, as these stories prove ...

———>➤●◄———

'Coincidence, if traced far enough back, becomes inevitable.'

ANON.

KEEPING IT IN THE FAMILY

Families, as we shall see on pp.203–213, have a funny way of coming together despite the circumstances that drive them apart. That said, in all but one of these stories the connection that unites the generations is of the cheerless rather than touching variety.

LIKE FATHER, LIKE SON

When martial arts actor Bruce Lee died mid-movie in 1973, producers were forced to cobble the film together by splicing footage of Lee with the work of two stand-ins. *Game of Death*, about a martial arts star who is shot and presumed killed by a prop gun containing a real bullet, was finally released in 1978.

In 1993, twenty years after Bruce Lee's death, his son Brandon, also a martial arts actor, was filming *The Crow* when he was accidentally shot and killed – by a prop gun containing a real bullet.

Runaway Train

Italian train driver Domenico Serafino must seriously have considered a career change – or preferably retirement – after accidentally hitting and killing two members of the public in accidents almost five years apart.

In January 1991, in poor visibility, his train had struck a car driven by nineteen-year-old Cristina Veroni on the Guastella–Reggio line. Then, in November 1995, Serafino was approaching the same crossing in the same train when he saw that a car had stopped on the tracks ahead of him. He slammed on the brakes but it was too late.

By grim coincidence, the driver of the second car was Vittorio Veroni, Cristina's father.

————◦————

Uneasy Rider

In July 1974, seventeen-year-old Neville Ebbin was riding his moped in Hamilton, Bermuda, when he was hit by a taxi and killed. One year later, in July 1975, his younger brother Erskine, now seventeen himself, was killed in an identical accident. That is, *entirely* identical: same moped, same road, same taxi, same taxi driver – and even the same taxi passenger.

———➤●◄———

STRUCK DOWN

In 1929 a young man was struck and killed by a bolt of lightning in his garden in Taranto, Italy. It was exactly the same spot in which his father had been killed by lightning in 1899. Ten years later, his own son suffered the same fate, in the same spot.

———➤●◄———

NOTHING IF NOT PREDICTABLE

Doctors in Hampshire were surprised when they realized the little girl they had just delivered had been born at 12.12 on 12/12 in 1997, but for baby Emily's family the coincidence barely raised an eyebrow. Her grandmother had been born on 11/11, her father on 4/4 at 4.40, her mother on 10/10 and her brother on 6/6.

'For this to happen would normally be a million-to-one chance,' a spokesman of Ladbrokes bookmakers commented. 'But if this particular family wanted a bet, it would only be 20–1.'

COINCIDENTAL CROSSING

In 1965, fourteen-year-old David Whisler was tragically hit and killed by a car while crossing the Big Lagoon Bridge in Eureka, California. Six years earlier his grandfather Hiram Besinger had been crushed to death by a timber truck and two years before that his great-grandfather, Richard Besinger, had also been killed by a passing car – all on the same bridge.

NOT THE FIRST TIME

Do you believe in déjà vu?
  Do you believe in déjà vu?

——➤●◄——

JOINED IN DEATH

As two of the most iconic United States presidents, it is little wonder that Abraham Lincoln and John F. Kennedy should have much in common. But in one respect the similarities between them are quite unbelievable: the circumstances of their assassinations are almost identical.

Lincoln, who had been elected to Congress in 1846 and elected president in 1860, was killed in Ford's Theater. Kennedy, elected to Congress in 1946 and elected president in 1960, was killed in a Ford Lincoln. Both were shot in the head on a Friday and in the presence of their wives. Lincoln's assassin fled from the theatre and hid in a warehouse while Kennedy's did the opposite, fleeing from the Texas School Book Depository to the Texas Theater.

Both presidents' surnames contain seven letters. Both assassins were known by three names – John Wilkes Booth and Lee Harvey Oswald – and both were killed before they could be brought to trial.

The vice presidents who succeeded Lincoln and Kennedy were both Southerners named Johnson. Andrew Johnson was born in 1809, Lyndon B. Johnson in 1909.

'History is a relentless master. It has no present, only the past rushing into the future.'

JOHN F. KENNEDY

1066 AND ALL THAT

The D-Day invasion of Normandy proved a decisive campaign in the fight against Hitler, but, judging by a number of strange coincidences, it can also be seen as a very belated retaliation for the Norman invasion of Britain nine centuries earlier.

The Battle of Hastings took place in 1066; D-Day was 6/6. The former was partially commanded by Roger de Montgomerie, the latter by Field Marshal Bernard Montgomery. And the Battle of Hastings was fought on 14 October, which, in 1944, was not only the birthday of Supreme Allied Commander Dwight D. Eisenhower but also the date on which one of Hitler's best-known field marshals, Erwin Rommel, committed suicide.

SEEING DOUBLE

When Margaret Thatcher died in 1996, not a single foreign dignitary turned up for her funeral. The reason? This Margaret had been the first wife of Denis Thatcher, and had divorced him in 1948; his second wife, also Margaret, is the one who was the British prime minister from 1979 to 1990, and who died in 2013.

Copyright Chaos

Children on both sides of the Atlantic are familiar with the mischievous, red-clad cartoon character Dennis the Menace, who made his publication debut on 12 March 1951. But if asked to draw this character, the two sets of children would come up with significantly different images. Why? Because, in a coincidence that is less 'history repeating' than 'history happening in two places at once', two completely unrelated Dennis the Menace cartoons were premiered on either side of the Pond on exactly the same day.

In the States, Dennis the Menace was inspired by illustrator Hank Ketcham's son, Dennis, while in the UK he was inspired by the Music Hall song 'Dennis the Menace from Venice' and first doodled on the back of a cigarette packet by Ian Chisholm, editor of the *Beano* comic.

Both cartoons are still in regular syndication, although to avoid confusion the US version is simply called Dennis in the UK, and the UK version is now more commonly known as Dennis and Gnasher.

YOU AGAIN

Have you ever had the feeling someone's following you? These people certainly have ....

———►●◄———

Annual Visit

When Gordon White returned home to discover a car had smashed through his front window, repairs and redecoration were the last things on his mind. He was more incredulous as to how driver Eric Williams had managed to replicate the accident exactly a year to the day since he had last driven into Mr White's front room.

Williams, who had to admit to driving without a licence, had apparently blacked out on both occasions.

'I still can't believe it,' Mr White told reporters. 'It was bad enough the first time round, but for it to happen again, and by the same guy ... well, it's something from a movie script.'

He was unsurprised to see the same recovery man arrive to retrieve the ruined car from his front room, which was now once again in need of some urgent TLC.

'If I'd have known this would happen I'd have chosen cheaper wallpaper,' he sighed.

⟶➤●◄⟶

'Those who do not remember the
past are destined to repeat it.'

GEORGE SANTAYANA

⟶➤●◄⟶

International Monk of Mystery

In 1836 a young Austrian art student named Joseph Matthäus Aigner tried to hang himself. At the last moment a Capuchin monk, unknown to Aigner, found him and talked him down. Four years later, aged just twenty-two but well on his way to becoming a renowned portraitist, Aigner once more wanted to end things; once again he tried to hang himself and once again he was discovered and saved by the Capuchin monk. Then, in 1848, Aigner became embroiled in an ill-fated revolutionary movement in Vienna, for which he was court-martialled and sentenced to death. He was ultimately pardoned, however, by Prince Alfred of Windisch-Grätz, on the instigation of the very same monk.

Alas, when Aigner finally succeeded in committing suicide aged 68, the Capuchin monk was nowhere to be seen. But he was on hand to preside over the artist's funeral.

———◆———

'You can't connect the dots looking forward; you can only connect them looking backwards. So you have to trust that the dots will somehow connect in your future. You have to trust in something – your gut, destiny, life, karma, whatever.'

STEVE JOBS

———◆———

I Got You, Babe

Joseph Figlock, a Detroit street sweeper, was cleaning an alley in 1937 when a baby fell out of a fourth-floor window and landed on top of him. Both escaped unscathed – as indeed they both did a year later, when exactly the same thing happened again.

SOULMATES

WE'VE all given in to the temptation of googling our own names – let's not pretend – and been amused (and a little affronted) to find we are not entirely unique; other versions of us are out there doing all manner of weird and wonderful things. Or discovered in the course of polite party chitchat that we share a birthday or a cousin or an interest in beekeeping with a total stranger. One coincidence between separate lives is remarkable enough, but when one extraordinary parallel turns into a series of them it can be hard not to believe that it's fate rather than chance that connects us, as these stories reveal.

'If there were no such thing as coincidence, there would be no such word.'

HERON CARVIC

SEPARATED AT BIRTH?

Doppelgängers, identity mix-ups and utterly improbable synchronicity: surely the people involved in these tales of super-spooky similarities were destined to cross each other's paths when they did ...

ROYAL RESEMBLANCE

King Umberto I of Italy certainly had a meal to remember on 28 July 1900, when he and his entourage visited a small restaurant in the town of Monza. When the owner emerged to take his royal guest's order, Umberto found himself face to face with

a doppelgänger. Not only was the restaurateur almost identical to the king, but his name was also Umberto, his wife, like the queen, was called Margherita, and the restaurant itself had been opened on the day of the king's coronation. Chef Umberto died in a shooting the following day, just hours before King Umberto was shot and killed by an assassin.

THE TAXMAN COMETH

It's rare indeed for a tax bill to herald happy tidings but that is precisely what happened in 1983 to Patricia Ann Kern (née Campbell) of Colorado and Patricia Ann Di Biasi (née Campbell) of Oregon. When the former received a demand for $3,000 in unpaid taxes she phoned the Internal Revenue Service in alarm, telling them she had no recollection of the job for which she was being taxed, and indeed that she had never in her life been to Oregon. It gradually emerged that the two women had even more in common than their names: they were born on the same day, shared a social security number, both worked in bookkeeping and had fathers called Robert, husbands in the military and children of identical ages. Whether or not Mrs Di Biasi was as delighted as Mrs Kern to discover the mix-up is not recorded.

———————⟫●⟪———————

SEPARATED AT DEATH

When the family of unemployed labourer Albert Steer waved him off on his way from Kent to Surrey one morning in 1907, they little thought he might be found dead in central London the following day. But there was no doubt that the unfortunate fellow in the police description was Albert: he had one eye, a dented forehead and a gammy foot. The Steer children duly identified their father and he was solemnly laid to rest. Two months later, however, Albert appeared at the front door and cheerfully announced to his incredulous family that he had spent the summer earning money as a gardener in Surrey. Who, then, was the mysterious doppelgänger buried in Albert's grave? The case remains unsolved to this day.

———⇒●⇐———

Identity Theft

Over lunch 'al desko' one day, Jay Greening was idly flicking through a newspaper when he came to the job section and was struck by an advert for precisely the complex technical skills he possessed. Thinking this must be some sort of sign, he called the company to register his interest.

'That's great, Mr Greening,' said the recruiter. 'Could you come in for an interview at 3 p.m. on

Tues— Oh, hang on: I already have you down for 2.30. We just spoke!'

Utterly baffled, Jay insisted that he hadn't called earlier. Was it possible that someone else was trying to use his name and qualifications to get the job? In order to find out, he hatched a secret plan with the recruiter …

When the imposter arrived for his interview at 2.30 on the Thursday, the real Jay was ready and waiting. As the other man filled out his application form, Jay marched over and threw his own form down like a gauntlet: the two identical names were side by side. But far from fleeing the building, the other man just laughed in amazement – it really was just a bizarre coincidence! In an added twist, the two Jays had arrived on identical motorbikes.

———➤●◄———

GHOST TRAIN

In the 1920s, three Englishmen found themselves sharing an otherwise deserted carriage on a train travelling through Peru. As the hours passed and their silent contemplation of the landscape became rather monotonous, they struck up a polite conversation about Peru, England, and no doubt, the weather. After a while the first man introduced himself as Mr Bingham; the second was Mr Powell. And the third? Mr Bingham-Powell.

⟹➤●◄⟸

'Every single moment is a coincidence.'

DOUG COUPLAND

⟹➤●◄⟸

THE DATE RINGS A BELL

Bell-ringing is unsociably noisy work but when two Welsh campanologists finally managed to make themselves heard they discovered to their amusement that they shared a birthday, albeit in different years. But the really odd coincidence, they soon found, was that both had been born on their father's birthday – the fathers having been born on exactly the same date.

A FACEBOOK-TO-FACEBOOK MEETING

The wonders of social networking have put an end to the notion that we are all connected to each other by 'just' six degrees of separation. Nowadays a quick Internet search will call up the most distant of strangers in a matter of seconds. And so it was for Kelly Hildebrandt of Florida, who, bored one day at college, typed her own name into Facebook's search engine. She was surprised to find that there were indeed other people with the same name out there – most intriguingly, as one profile photo indicated, a topless young man from Texas. Female Kelly messaged male Kelly to remark on the coincidence and the two began an online friendship that ultimately led to them meeting in person.

'It felt like I'd known him my entire life,' said female Kelly of their first encounter at the airport. Having been raised in Christian households, both Kellys agreed that 'The Lord works in mysterious ways'.

But not mysterious enough, it would seem. Kelly and Kelly married in October 2009 but had filed for divorce by the summer of 2012 – only to face that most harrowing of modern break-up dilemmas: who would unfriend whom first?

'Man does not control his own fate.
The women in his life do that for
him.'

GROUCHO MARX

━━━━►●◄━━━

UNHAPPY CHRISTMAS

When it comes to strange coincidences between
two lives, identical twins have rather an unfair
advantage. Nonetheless, certain pairs seem prone to
eerier synchronization than others. Take Lorraine
and Levinia Christmas of Norfolk, who both, on the
spur of the moment, decided to drive to one another's
houses to deliver presents on Christmas Eve 1994. The
country road between their villages was precariously
icy, however, and both sisters were involved in a head-
on crash – with each other. They ultimately spent
Christmas in the same hospital as their father – Father
Christmas? – who was recovering from surgery.

━━━━►●◄━━━

After You

Eerier yet are the many tales of identical twins dying on the same day and often unbeknownst to each other. In 2002, two Finnish brothers in their seventies died within hours of one another in separate accidents on the same road near the town of Raahe, north of Helsinki.

'This is simply a historic coincidence,' police officer Marja-Leena Huhtala later commented. 'It made my hair stand on end when I heard the two were brothers, and identical twins at that. It came to mind that perhaps someone from upstairs had a say in this.'

Meanwhile in Perth, Australia, 61-year-old identical twins John and William Bloomfield both died of heart attacks within minutes of each other while watching a body-building contest at a casino. A police spokesman noted that the brothers had been inseparable and had never lived apart: 'Police who attended the home found identical pairs of everything. All their clothes were in sets of two.'

SUPER-IDENTICAL TWINS

In the summer of 1939, the Lewis family and the Springer family of Ohio both adopted baby boys, and both sets of parents named their new son James. Unbeknownst to either family, the Jameses were in fact identical twins who had been separated at birth. It was only thanks to a clerical error six years later that Mrs Lewis discovered her son had a brother, but it was not until the boys were forty years old that James Lewis contacted James Springer with the news. After the initial shock of their separation and reunion had passed, the brothers found that they had much more in common than a shared name and genetic code. They had both married women called Linda, had sons named James Alan, then divorced Linda and married Betty. Both were keen carpenters and trained police officers, and both had a dog named Toy.

⟫●⟪

DREAM HOUSE

A house-buyer in Scotland was delighted to receive the keys to his new property in the mail, but suddenly remembered he hadn't asked the seller about the security code for the alarm. He called him to ask and was told it was 1405.

'Funny,' said the buyer. 'That's my birthday.'

'Mine too!' cried the seller.

———➤●◄———

If the Name Fits ...

During the course of a routine appointment, a doctor asked his new patient about her unusual surname. She explained that it was Scandinavian and so rare that nobody she met had ever heard of it.

'Interesting you should say that,' said the doctor, 'because one of my nurses has almost the same name – different spelling.'

The patient was amazed by the coincidence but thought nothing more of it as she made her way home. As she opened her front door, however, the phone was ringing, and the man on the other end – calling from Germany – explained that he had been looking for an old acquaintance of a similar name and had dialled the only comparable entry in the phone book.

'You're in luck!' said the woman. 'I can even tell you where she works.'

You've Got Mail

While on a business trip in Louisville, Kentucky, George D. Bryson checked himself in to the Brown Hotel. During his stay he asked the receptionist whether there was any post for him and sure enough there was a letter marked 'George D. Bryson, room 307'.

But the letter wasn't for him. It was for the previous occupant of room 307, a Canadian businessman named George D. Bryson.

A DATE WITH DESTINY

Woody Allen once noted that 'Time is nature's way of keeping everything from happening at once', but there are certain dates in history with more than their fair share of momentous events. Take these uncanny famous pairings who entered or exited the world on exactly the same day as each other: is it mere coincidence or was there a greater force at work?

———————⟫●⟪———————

Born on the Same Day

12 February 1809: Charles Darwin and
Abraham Lincoln

It seems fitting that two men who made such important contributions to human civilization – Darwin the theory of evolution and Lincoln the abolition of slavery – should have been born on the same day. As boys they both struggled academically but they were later able to change the course of history by staying true to their convictions despite considerable opposition. Things might have turned out a little differently if the two men had died on the same day, though: Darwin had not yet published *The Descent of Man*, his controversial work on our ape ancestors, by the time Lincoln was assassinated in April 1865.

6 July 1946: Sylvester Stallone and George W. Bush

One of them is an oft-parodied tough guy with a formidable mother and a funny way of talking, best known for his role as the triumphant underdog with a taste for revenge, and the other (you know where this is going) is Sylvester Stallone. Yes, in what seems like some sort of cosmic joke, Rocky and Dubya were born on the same day. Both came from dubious pasts – Stallone's soft-core pornography, Bush's alcoholism – to achieve notoriety, but have rather fallen from grace since their heyday. Also born on the same day is Professor Peter Singer, animal-rights activist and author of *The President of Good and Evil: The Ethics of George W. Bush*.

6 July 1935: Candy Barr and the Dalai Lama

Sharing a birthday but not a birth date with Stallone and Bush are these polar opposites: one a notorious stripper, burlesque dancer and drug-user and the other the hallowed spiritual leader of Tibet. When the Dalai Lama, a fervent supporter of women's rights, said the next holder of his position might well be a woman, it is unlikely that he had his birthday twin in mind.

3 April 1924: Marlon Brando and Doris Day

At first glance there seems to be very little in common between the mumbling Hollywood rebel – the Godfather himself – and the sweet-voiced national treasure whose 'Sentimental Journey' welcomed American troops home from World War II. Both descended from German ancestors, Brando grew up in Evanston, Illinois while Day was born in Evanston, Ohio – and both caught their big break in 1944. In later life, both ruffled feathers with their outspoken political activism, Day corralling other Hollywood royalty into supporting her crusade against animal cruelty and Brando sending an Apache woman onto the stage to decline his 1973 Best Actor Oscar as a statement against the depiction of Native Americans in the movies.

DEAR SIR

Monty Python star Eric Idle and Conservative politician John Major were both born on 29 March 1943. In 1993, Idle wrote to Major, then Prime Minister, to wish him a happy fiftieth birthday. 'Has it ever occurred to you,' he wrote, 'that, but for a twist of fate, I should be Prime Minister and you could have been the Man in the Nudge Nudge sketch from Monty Python? I do hope you don't feel too disappointed. Happy birthday anyway.'

21 October 1940: Geoffrey Boycott and Pele

Nike, the goddess of victory, must have been looking down from the heavens on this auspicious date to witness the births of a legendary cricketer and a legendary footballer. Although they were born on opposite sides of the world, both Boycott and Pele grew up in impoverished circumstances and only escaped a lifetime of hardship thanks to their extraordinary will to succeed. Young Pele earned his pocket money as a teahouse servant and practised his footwork in his spare time using a stuffed sock in lieu of a ball. Young Boycott, the son of a miner, had his spleen removed after a near-fatal accident aged eight and was initially a mediocre cricketer due to poor sight. He went on to become one of the most successful batsmen in cricketing history, while Pele is widely recognized as the greatest footballer of the twentieth century.

⊰●⊱

Died on the Same Day

4 July 1826: John Adams and Thomas Jefferson

It is coincidence enough that two founding fathers and former American presidents should die on the same day, but that they should do so on Independence Day, exactly fifty years after co-signing the Declaration of Independence, beggars belief. The two men had been both friends and rivals during their political careers but the final words uttered by John Adams on his deathbed were 'Thomas Jefferson survives'. He was incorrect, of course: Jefferson had beaten him to the afterlife by a matter of hours. Unbelievably, former president James Monroe died on the same date just five years later.

22 November 1963: John F. Kennedy, Aldous Huxley and C. S. Lewis

Two giants of British literature, authors of the timeless classics *Brave New World* and the Narnia series, died on the very same day and hardly anyone noticed: the staggering assassination of JFK that afternoon commandeered news headlines until long after they were laid to rest.

11 October 1963: Jean Cocteau and Edith Piaf

Just six weeks before the curiously intertwined deaths of two British literary greats, a similar fate befell the Parisian arts world when the legendary director and the troubled national treasure passed away on the same day. Cocteau and Piaf had long been friends and moved in the same circles – his critically acclaimed 1940 play *Le Bel Indifférent* was written for and starred Piaf – and indeed it is said that he died of heart failure after hearing of her death. A final numerological coincidence is that he was 74 and she was 47.

30 January 1948: Orville Wright and Mahatma Gandhi

The aviation pioneer and co-inventor of the first practical aeroplane died on the same day as the civil-rights campaigner and hero of Indian independence. Despite appearances, the two high-fliers (sorry) in their respective fields had one other big thing in common in that they died in unexpected ways. Wright, who spent much of his life flying rickety planes, died of a heart attack while on the ground; Gandhi, whose peaceful protests included hunger strikes and threats of suicide, was ultimately assassinated.

3 February 1959: Buddy Holly, The Big Bopper, and Ritchie Valens

Arguably less of a coincidence than a terrible tragedy, the plane crash that killed three such talented young musicians quickly became seen as an act of cruel fate. Indeed, in his 1971 hit 'American Pie', Don McLean immortalized 3 February 1959 as 'the day the music died'.

'You often meet your fate on the
road you take to avoid it.'

GOLDIE HAWN

A BIRTHDAY TO REMEMBER

Statistically speaking you're surely as likely to die on
your birthday as on any other day of the year (perhaps
even more so after one too many celebratory drinks),
yet it remains a surprisingly rare occurrence – with a
few notable exceptions.

23 April 1564–23 April 1616: William Shakespeare
Coincidentally, the date on which England's most famous
son entered and exited the world is also St George's Day.

18 July 1895–18 July 1954: George 'Machine Gun' Kelly
One of America's most notorious Prohibition-era
bootleggers and gangsters, Kelly died not in a dramatic
shoot-out but of a heart attack in prison, where he
had spent almost half his life.

29 August 1915–29 August 1982: Ingrid Bergman
The striking actress who uttered one of the most
misquoted lines in celluloid history ('Play it, Sam. Play
"As Time Goes By"') died in London but had her ashes
scattered off the coast of her native Sweden.

DIVINE INTERVENTIONS

You don't have to be religious to sense from time to time that an incredible stroke of luck, a victory against all the odds, has happened because someone is watching over you. From portentous dreams to holy visions, here are some real-life parables that suggest we are indeed in the hands of the gods.

'Trifles light as air
Are to the jealous confirmations strong
As proofs of holy writ.'

SHAKESPEARE, *OTHELLO*

MAY THE BEST MAN WIN

The history books are full of inexplicable victories and military turnarounds founded on the most unlikely circumstances – could they be a sign from above that one side is favoured over the other?

━━━━➢●◁━━━━

FROM RUSSIA WITHOUT LOVE

Encountering snow in a Russian midwinter is nothing out of the ordinary, but that identical weather events should thwart two of the biggest attempted invasions in history – led by two of the most famous military leaders of all time, at the height of their power – is rather more bizarre.

Napoleon Bonaparte's Grande Armée marched into Russia in the summer of 1812 in what was supposed to be a decisive victory – which it was, for the Russians. Having wildly underestimated both how long it would take 400,000 men to march to Moscow and how much equipment, food, animal feed and season-appropriate clothing would be needed to get there and back, the French forces found themselves in the depths of a Russian winter without any hope of surviving it. At one stage Napoleon was losing 5,000 men per day and 80 horses per mile; only a quarter of his men made it to Moscow and just a fraction of that number made it back to Paris.

In an eerily similar tale set 129 years later, Adolf Hitler attempted much the same thing and achieved much the same result. Once again entering Russia during summer with expectations of a swift victory, this time the invading army numbered almost 4 million. Having underestimated the might of the Russian forces and the horrors of the Russian winter, the Germans finally reached the outskirts of Moscow just in time to be hit by particularly severe winter blizzards. The supply of fuel to the front had been prioritized over food and clothing, and much of that fuel ended up in heaters rather than vehicles. With 1 million men killed or wounded and 5,000 planes and tanks destroyed, Hitler was forced, like Napoleon, to retreat.

'Providence has its appointed hour
for everything.'

MAHATMA GANDHI

———➤●◄———

A DIVINE WIND

A lesser-known but considerably more remarkable
meteorological coincidence befell the great Kublai
Khan, Mongol emperor and founder of China's Yuan
Dynasty, when he attempted, twice, to conquer Japan
in the late thirteenth century.

After two letters requesting that the Imperial Court
simply surrender to the Mongol Empire were returned
with a polite 'thanks but no thanks', Kublai Khan
vowed to overwhelm Japan with his military might.
In 1274 he sent over 20,000 soldiers in 800 ships to
take the Japanese island of Kyushu – which they did,
for a few hours, until a sudden typhoon whipped up
around them and forced the Mongols back to the sea,
where most of them drowned.

Not to be outdone, Kublai Khan tried a similar
tactic seven years later, in 1281, but this time tried to

outwit the Japanese with a vastly bigger two-pronged attack: 40,000 men approached from one direction in 900 ships while 100,000 took another route in 3,500 ships. Once again they converged on Kyushu and made initial progress, until another almighty typhoon drove them back to the sea, where most of them were killed in the storm.

The Japanese invented a name for these two freak typhoons: kamikaze, or 'divine wind'. Kublai Khan wisely took the hint and never tried to invade Japan again.

———————>●<———————

Holy Smoke

In September 1862, at the height of the American Civil War, Confederate Army General Robert E. Lee issued a strategy document to the generals he had charged with capturing Maryland. Special Order 191, as it was known, gave specific movement orders for each unit and outlined battle plans that would result in a resounding victory for the South.

One of the copies of SO191 went to Major General

Stonewall Jackson, who in turn copied it for General Daniel Harvey Hill – who wrapped the paper around three cigars and stuffed them in an envelope to keep dry. In this function at least, SO191 fulfilled its purpose: a few days later, when a Union Army command set up camp in a field recently vacated by Hill, the package was lying in the grass, the document dry and legible, and with three free cigars to boot.

SO191 was passed up the ranks until it reached Union Army General George B. McClellan. He used the intelligence to attack Confederate forces in what became the Battle of Antietam, notorious as both the bloodiest day of battle ever fought in the United States and also an important strategic win for the ultimately victorious North.

———➤●◄———

DIVINE DISPATCHES

Have you ever had the feeling that the universe is trying to tell you something? Listen more closely next time – it may have a point.

———➤●◄———

GOOD ADVICE

In a case that must have been difficult for sceptical science journalists to write about, the 20 December 1997 edition of the esteemed *British Medical Journal* reported that a woman had undergone an operation for a brain tumour after being alerted to the condition by voices in her head.

The woman, known only as AB in the article, had moved to Britain from mainland Europe in the 1960s. She had never suffered particularly bad health until the winter of 1984, when she was interrupted while reading by a voice that said: 'Please don't be afraid. I know it must be shocking for you to hear me speaking to you like this, but this is the easiest way I could think of. My friend and I used to work at the Children's Hospital, Great Ormond Street, and we would like to help you.'

The voices went on to tell AB that she had a brain tumour and should go to a hospital at once, which she did. With considerable reluctance, given her total lack of symptoms, the doctors agreed to perform a brain scan – and sure enough AB had a brain tumour.

After a successful operation to remove the tumour, AB was visited by the voices one last time.

'We are pleased to have helped you,' they said. 'Goodbye.'

NOT AMUSED

Most critics gave Mel Gibson's controversial 2004 epic *The Passion of the Christ* carefully considered write-ups, but one unimpressed viewer pulled no punches in giving it an almighty thumbs-down: God himself.

During filming just outside Rome, actor Jim Caviezel – in the role of Jesus – was struck by a sudden bolt of lightning.

'I'm about a hundred feet away,' producer Steve McEveety later told *Variety*, 'when I glance over and see smoke coming out of Caviezel's ears.'

The heavenly flame also smote assistant director Jan Michelini, who had been similarly rebuked just days earlier while holding an umbrella during a storm. Fortunately neither man was injured and the show was able to go on.

A PLAGUE ON ALL OUR HOUSES

In the Book of Exodus in the Bible, God smites the Egyptian Pharaoh with ten increasingly gruesome plagues – from blood to death, via frogs, lice and locusts – to compel him to release the Israelites from slavery. But such heaven-sent pestilences are sadly not confined to the Old Testament. Indeed, they have been occurring with increasing regularity in recent decades.

In October 1947, minnows and black bass – all fresh but dead – fell on Biloxi, Mississippi during a rainstorm. Ten years later thousands of crayfish fell on Thomasville, Alabama. A similar phenomenon was reported in east London in May 1984, when fish identified by the Natural History Museum as flounder and smelt fell from the sky. In May 1996, two dozen recently deceased fish dropped on Hatfield, Hertfordshire, and two years later Croydon was pelted with dead frogs. Tadpoles fell on Ishikawa Prefecture in Japan throughout June 2009 and the small Hungarian town of Rákóczifalva was struck twice by amphibians in June 2010.

Even more alarming are reports of falling worms in Jennings, Louisiana in July 2007 and a shower of spiders in Salta Province, Argentina, in April that same year.

Is this all just a bizarre fluke or should we be taking note?

Opinions from On High

Much like Elvis Presley, both Jesus Christ and the Virgin Mary seem to spend much of their time appearing to people in unlikely places – more often than not on slices of toasted bread. In 2004, Diane Duyser of Florida sold her ten-year-old toasted cheese sandwich bearing the face of the Virgin Mary to a casino for $28,000.

But what of the instances where these visions appear to hundreds or thousands of people? Are they divine messages or just a trick of the light?

Between 1968 and 1971 the Virgin Mary appeared repeatedly on the roof of an Orthodox church in Zeitoun, Egypt, where she was deemed by thousands of pilgrims to be bringing a message of peace following the Six Day War. In June 2003 a condensation stain that resembled Mary holding the infant Jesus appeared on the window of Milton Hospital in Boston, drawing tens of thousands of believers, many of whom saw it as an anti-abortion message from above.

But when, in 2007, a woman from Surrey claimed the Virgin Mary had been appearing in a pine tree in her garden with a similar anti-abortion message for over twenty years, the Vatican was having none of it. Archbishop Angelo Amato of the Congregation of the Doctrine of the Faith dismissed the 'Our Lady of Surbiton' visions as 'hysterical'.

JOIN THE CLUB

For many decades, an intriguing trend for talented musicians to die at the age of twenty-seven seemed nothing more than a tragic coincidence: among them blues singer Robert Johnson (1938), Rolling Stone Brian Jones (1969), Jimi Hendrix and Janis Joplin (1970) and Ron McKernan of the Grateful Dead (1973). But following the death aged twenty-seven of Nirvana frontman Kurt Cobain in 1994, the notion of a doomed – or hallowed, depending on how you look at it – '27 Club' was born. More recent members include Richey Edwards of the Manic Street Preachers, who went missing, presumed dead, in 1995, and Amy Winehouse, who died in 2011.

Heavenly Creatures

On a wet and misty night in the late nineteenth century, a train carrying hundreds of passengers was speeding its way towards London. As the driver peered out at the murky landscape unfolding before him, a tall man in a dark cape appeared from nowhere. He was standing on the tracks, waving frantically for the train to stop.

Acting quickly, the driver brought the train to a sudden halt just ahead of where the man had been standing – but when he got out there was nobody there. He and his engineers ran along the track a

short way but had to stop abruptly: a bridge the train had been due to cross was badly storm-damaged and partially collapsed. Without the intervention of this mysterious figure, they would all surely have died.

Was it a heavenly messenger who saved everyone that evening? Perhaps, albeit in an unusual form ... A few days later, one of the engineers noticed an enormous dead moth stuck at the base of one of the train's headlights. He spread its wings and pressed it against the light, and then switched the bulb on: sure enough, the tall, dark-caped figure appeared in the beam.

———⇒●⇐———

'There are no mistakes, no coincidences. All events are blessings given to us to learn from.'

ELISABETH KÜBLER-ROSS

———⇒●⇐———

Mysterious Ways

The Lord worked in a mysterious way indeed in Beatrice, Nebraska on 1 March 1950 when, by some unaccountable coincidence, all fifteen members of the local choir turned up late for practice and thereby escaped a gruesome death.

Choir practice at the church was due to start, as usual, at 7.20 p.m. and most members tended to arrive around 7.15, but by 7.25 not a single person, including the choirmaster, had yet turned up. Fortunate for them, for it was at this moment that a leak of natural gas was ignited by the church's furnace and the entire building exploded and collapsed.

The reasons for this mass tardiness are almost as bizarre as the story itself: six people were simply late because they uncharacteristically lost track of time; one was called away on a last-minute errand; two girls wanted to hear the end of a radio programme; sisters whose car wouldn't start asked another choir member for a lift but had to wait for her to finish her geometry homework; and the reverend and his family were detained by the daughter's sudden urge to iron her dress.

Prayers were no doubt said rather more fervently in Nebraska that evening.

'I cannot, if I am in the field of
glory, be kept out of sight: wherever
there is anything to be done, there
Providence is sure to direct my steps.'

HORATIO NELSON

———➣●ᶜ———

THAT'LL BE 10 PER CENT, THANKS

When the usual gobbledegook of our dreams is replaced with material that not only makes sense but also inspires great creativity, one has to wonder whether our nightly visions really are just random – or whether the seeds of ideas are purposely planted.

———➣●ᶜ———

MAGICAL MYSTERY DREAM

One morning in 1965, Paul McCartney awoke from a dream with a tune in his head. The Beatles were in the middle of recording their album *Help!* so he rushed over to his piano and played the song a few times so as not to forget it.

'I liked the melody a lot,' he later recalled, 'but because I'd dreamed it, I couldn't believe I'd written it … For about a month I went round to people in the music business and asked them whether they had ever heard it before.'

Convinced eventually that he had indeed composed the whole song whilst unconscious, McCartney and John Lennon began adding lyrics to the tune. It seems divine inspiration struck once again when the original first line – 'Scrambled eggs … Oh, my baby, how I love your legs' – was replaced with the eminently more touching 'Yesterday … All my troubles seemed so far away …'

'Those who have succeeded at anything and don't mention luck are kidding themselves.'

LARRY KING

NIGHT TERRORS

On an unseasonably gloomy summer's evening in 1816, the poet Lord Byron was hosting his literary friends Percy Bysshe Shelley and Mary Shelley at his villa beside Lake Geneva. After spooking one another by reading ghost stories around the fire, the Shelleys accepted Byron's challenge to compose their own scary tales.

That night, Mary Shelley couldn't sleep, but her head was full of terrifying half-dreams, as she later related in the introduction to the novel they inspired:

'I saw – with shut eyes, but acute mental vision – I saw … the hideous phantasm of a man stretched out, and then, on the working of some powerful engine, show signs of life, and stir with an uneasy, half-vital motion … I could not so easily get rid of my hideous phantom; still it haunted me. I must try to think of something else. I recurred to my ghost story – my tiresome, unlucky ghost story! O! if I could only contrive one which would frighten my reader as I myself had been frightened that night! … On the morrow I announced that I had *thought of a story*. I began that day with the words, "It was on a dreary night of November", making only a transcript of the grim terrors of my waking dream.'

The novel that unravelled before the terrified nineteen-year-old was *Frankenstein*, one of the most famous stories ever composed.

HEAVENLY HAIRCARE

Proving perhaps that his nocturnal tips are not limited to the creative arts, at the turn of the twentieth century God helped a young black entrepreneur become the first female self-made millionaire in the United States.

Sarah Walker, who went by the name of Madam C. J. Walker, had long suffered from hair loss and scalp disease, both common issues for poor women of the period with inadequate access to washing facilities. After much trial and error with various concoctions of her own design, she prayed for divine inspiration.

'He answered my prayer,' she later revealed, 'for one night I had a dream, and in that dream a big black man appeared to me and told me what to mix up in my hair. Some of the remedy was grown in Africa, but I sent for it, mixed it, put it on my scalp, and in a few weeks my hair was coming in faster than it had ever fallen out. I tried it on my friends; it helped them. I made up my mind to begin to sell it.'

From small beginnings advising other black women how to look after their hair, Madam C. J. Walker's haircare empire grew steadily, and she died the wealthiest African-American woman in the country, if not the world.

CREEPY COINCIDENCES

For every coincidence that makes us laugh and think 'Fancy that!' there's another that sends a shiver down our spines: a string of misfortune that can surely only be a curse, jinx or paranormal occurrence.

'Coincidence is the word we use when we can't see the levers and pulleys.'

EMMA BULL

DOOMED TO FAILURE

It is a truth universally acknowledged that 'bad things happen in threes'; for many of us, one minor mishap foretells an entire day spent pessimistically awaiting the inevitable onslaught of further bad luck. But can these bone-chilling jinxes from the world of entertainment really be brushed off as coincidence rather than curse?

MACBETH

Even the most cynical of actors would think twice about referring to Shakespeare's chilling work about thwarted ambition and witches' curses as anything other than 'The Scottish Play'. Why? Because ~~Macbeth~~ the play has suffered what can only be described as an unparalleled level of catastrophe since it first appeared in 1606. Over the centuries it has been suggested that the play itself is haunted, either by the violent ghost of Banquo – an ancestor of James VI, for whom Shakespeare wrote it, but whose murderous character was glossed over in order to please the king – or by spells cast by 'witches' of the early seventeenth century who were angry at Shakespeare's portrayal of their ancient craft.

Whatever the cause of the curse of *Macbeth*, the play was doomed from its opening night, when the boy playing Lady M succumbed to a deadly fever, leaving Shakespeare to play the part himself. Since then, and in theatres all over the world, Lady Macbeth has variously been strangled, mobbed or injured, or fallen off stage during the sleepwalking scene, while Macbeth has inexplicably lost his voice mid-performance, or collapsed and been hospitalized, or, in one horrifically dramatic turn of events in Amsterdam in 1672, actually stabbed and killed King Duncan with a real knife substituted for the fake. Laurence Olivier almost met an untimely demise in 1937 when a stage weight fell from the rigging, John Gielgud's 1942 production witnessed the deaths of King Duncan and two witches, and Charlton Heston donned tights accidentally soaked in kerosene in 1953 and suffered severe burns to his groin and legs.

But by far the most violent manifestation of the curse occurred in New York on 10 May 1869, when two rival actors played rival performances of *Macbeth* just a few blocks apart and sparked what became known as the Astor Place Riot, in which thirty-one of their supporters were trampled to death. The two actors had previous form, though, having publicly argued about who was better at playing the great roles of Shakespeare – notably (you guessed it) Macbeth.

'GLOOMY SUNDAY'

On a bleak Sunday in December 1932, with the clouds hanging ominously low over Paris, a struggling Hungarian composer sat down at his piano to write a song. Short on cash and unlucky in love, Rezso Seress poured his gloom into the melancholy tune, which he aptly entitled 'End of the World'. After a poet friend of his had added some suitably depressing lyrics, the song was renamed 'Gloomy Sunday'. Alas, the composer's mood was not brightened by the feedback he received from the first music publisher to whom he sent it: 'There is a sort of terrible compelling despair about it. I don't think it would do anyone any good to hear a song like that.'

His second submission was successful, however, and the composition was printed and distributed across Europe. It was not until 1936 that the song made any great impact, and even then it was the sort of exposure Seress could happily have lived without: linked to a spate of suicides in his native Hungary, 'Gloomy Sunday' became known as 'the Hungarian suicide song' and was banned there. In Berlin, a young shop assistant was said to have hanged herself after listening to it, while a young man shot himself in a 'Gloomy Sunday'-induced depression. In Rome, a teenager jumped to his death from a bridge.

But they say all publicity is good publicity, and indeed the now-notorious song was quickly translated into English and recorded by a number of artists in the United States – where its deadly curse soon took hold. An elderly New Yorker leapt from his window after playing the tune on his piano, while a secretary in the same city gassed herself, her final request that the song be played at her funeral. In London, a woman was found dead from an overdose after her record player malfunctioned and repeated the same gloomy refrain over and over.

None of this seems to have warned more recent recording artists off the compellingly miserable song

– among them Marianne Faithfull, Sarah Brightman and Sinead O'Connor – but the depressing coda to this already tragic tale is that Rezso Seress killed himself by jumping out of a Budapest window in January 1968.

⟹➤●◄⟸

SUPERMAN

The curse that supposedly hangs over the role of Superman is almost as famous as the superhero's dashing blue tights, and a number of actors – among them Jude Law and Josh Hartnett – have even turned down lucrative lead-role offers in film adaptations of the comic.

The series of uncanny tragedies dates back to the earliest Superman actors in the 1940s. Bud Collyer, who was the voice of Superman for the first cartoons between 1941 and 1943, and again in 1966, died of a circulatory condition at just 61; Superman no. 2, Kirk Alyn, blamed his 1940s stint as Superman for his subsequent typecasting and the demise of his career – by 1978 he was still stuck in the Superman rut, by now demoted to playing Lois Lane's father – and he died after a long affliction with Alzheimer's. Another veteran of the 1978 movie, Lee Quigley, who played baby Superman, died aged just 14 from solvent abuse.

The two best-known victims of the Curse of Superman coincidentally – or as fate decreed it – share eerily similar names: George Reeves, who played the role in the early 1950s, died after apparently shooting himself days before he was due to get married in 1959, although his fingerprints were not on the gun lying beside his body ... while Christopher Reeve, hero of the ill-fated 1978 movie and its 1980s sequels, was paralyzed from the neck down in a horse riding accident, the effects of which ultimately killed him in 2004.

Of course there are other Supermen who seem impervious to the curse – notably Dean Cain – but it does appear to strike when the actors least expect it. Bob Holiday, a 1966 musical Superman, is still waiting, and even tempted fate in 2012, aged 79, by declaring, 'I think the idea of a "Superman Curse" is silly. Look at me, I'm still here. I have had nothing but good come from me playing Superman. Life is good, and I'm having a ball' ...

THE EXORCIST

Banned in a number of countries for its graphic content, the groundbreaking horror movie *The Exorcist* (1973) is said to have been cursed from the outset. The writer of the original book and subsequent screenplay, William Peter Blatty, director William Friedkin and lead actress Ellen Burstyn have all commented on the series of strange occurrences during and after filming – most notably the studio fire that destroyed all the house-interior sets except for the child's bedroom, in which the chief creepiness (and most iconic scene) occurs.

According to Friedkin, a priest was brought in numerous times to bless the set and assuage the fears of those working on it. Burstyn received a back injury during a stunt in one of the film's most notoriously disturbing scenes, as did Linda Blair in the role of Regan, during a scene in which she was supposedly possessed by devils. Those with a particularly macabre mindset also suggest that the death (from influenza) of Irish actor Jack MacGowran shortly after he filmed his role as director Burke Dennings, who is killed in the film, is not entirely coincidental.

Depending on whom you ask, between four and nine people died while filming was underway or shortly thereafter. Good for publicity; not so good for the unfortunate souls involved.

'I never believed that anything was a coincidence. There's a reason for everything that happens.'

ELVIS PRESLEY

UNLUCKY 13

Triskaidekaphobia, or fear of the number 13, is so widespread the world over that even the most cynical people will go to great lengths to avoid it. But is there really anything to this supposed curse or has the number simply got a bad press as a result of a series of (admittedly rather creepy) coincidences? Let's examine the evidence …

Come Dine With Me

Arguably the most famous dinner party in history, the Last Supper, had thirteen guests, including Jesus. Some Christians even believe that the traitor Judas was the thirteenth guest to take his seat, just in time to hear Christ prophesy that 'One of you shall betray me ... The hand of him that betrayeth me is with me on the table ...'

But the Last Supper was not the first ill-fated religious meal. Norse mythology tells of a banquet at Valhalla to which twelve gods were invited, but which Loki, the god of mischief and the thirteenth god in the Norse Pantheon, gatecrashed. With thirteen guests now present, all hell broke loose: Loki encouraged the blind god Hodur to murder Baldur the Good using an arrow made of mistletoe – and was subsequently the thirteenth 'mourner' to arrive at Baldur's funeral.

A SILENT GUEST

The curse of having thirteen guests to dinner continues into the modern day, or so the management of London's exclusive Savoy Hotel seems to believe. Since 1926, any gathering of thirteen people at the hotel is joined by a silent fourteenth guest: Kaspar the wooden black cat, a three-foot-high sculpture specially created for the hotel by artist Basil Ionides. If Kaspar is attending a sit-down dinner, he is even

given a seat, a serviette, a full place setting and a three-course meal.

The origin of this precaution at the Savoy is a dinner party that was held there in 1898 by South African businessman Woolf Joel. Due to a last-minute cancellation, the fourteen-guest gathering was reduced to thirteen, and talk turned to the unlucky number; some of those present believed that the first person to leave the table would suffer some dreadful misfortune. Joel apparently laughed this off – but was shot dead upon his return to his Johannesburg office.

The hotel initially assuaged the superstitious fears of its guests by ensuring a member of staff remained in any room containing thirteen people, but the sensitive nature of many of the conversations taking place at high-powered gatherings made it preferable for the fourteenth guest to have ears made of wood.

When not attending formal functions, Kaspar sits in a glass cabinet and keeps watch over the hotel gift shop.

LUCK OF THE IRISH

In 2013 the Irish government took extraordinary measures to stave off the bad luck associated with the number thirteen by making an unprecedented amendment to the country's vehicle-registration system.

Normally a car registered in, say, 2012 would have a registration number beginning '12', but fears that Irish car dealerships would take a financial hit from having their lots filled with vehicles marked '13' led to a ruling that licence plates from the first half of the year would begin '131' and those from the second half of the year would begin '132'.

> 'We must believe in luck. For how else can we explain the success of those we don't like?'
>
> JEAN COCTEAU

FLIGHT FRIGHT

Frequent flyers may have noticed that a number of airlines do not have a row 13. While one of these airlines, Reno Air, claims that it wants to avoid any passengers feeling unlucky as they take off for the casinos of Reno, other international carriers – among them Lufthansa, Air France, Iberia and Ryanair – seemingly omit the row out of a less specific sense of doom.

In 2007, fear of the cursed number forced one new airline to redesign its logo just days after unveiling it. Brussels Airlines originally had a 'b' logo made up, coincidentally, of thirteen dots, but quickly added a fourteenth after being inundated with complaints from terrified would-be passengers.

Spokesman Geert Sciot commented that passengers 'think it brings them bad luck. We are never surprised by reactions – but that it was that bad? It really took us aback.'

FRIDAY 13

Taking the phobia of the number thirteen one step further, paraskevidekatriaphobia is a specific fear of Friday 13. This superstition supposedly dates back to Friday 13 October 1307, when King Philip IV of France ordered the mass arrests of hundreds of Knights Templar and then had them falsely charged with – and executed for – all manner of heretical practices.

The passing of over 800 years has done nothing to quell fears of Friday 13. Indeed, a 2004 study estimated that US businesses lose around $900 million every time the unlucky combination comes round due to superstitions about travelling, moving or getting married on such an inauspicious date. Meanwhile, in 1993, the *British Medical Journal* published a study that compared the number of vehicles using Britain's busiest motorway on Friday 13 with the number of hospital admissions due to accidents. Its conclusions make for chilling reading:

'There were consistently and significantly fewer vehicles on the southern section of the M25 on Friday the 13th compared with Friday the 6th. Admissions due to transport accidents were significantly increased on Friday the 13th. Friday the 13th is unlucky for some. The risk of hospital admission as a result of a transport accident may be increased by as much as 52%. Staying at home is recommended.'

And transport disasters on Friday 13 have not been limited to the roads. In 1972, two notorious aeroplane crashes occurred on Friday 13 October. One was the crash-landing of a Soviet Aeroflot jet that killed all 174 people on board, and which was at that time the deadliest airline accident the world had ever seen. The second, which occurred within hours of the Russian catastrophe, was the crash of Uruguayan Air Force Flight 571 in freezing conditions high up in the Andes. Of the forty-five people on board, twelve died immediately and most of the survivors succumbed to frostbite, their injuries, avalanches or – as anyone who has seen the 1993 film *Alive* will recall

MUSICAL MYSTERY

Friday 13 has proven particularly unlucky for musicians, an inordinate number of whom have died on this date. They include Gioachino Rossini (13 November 1868), Arnold Schoenberg (13 July 1951), Benny Goodman (13 June 1986), Chet Baker (13 May 1988) and Tupac Shakur (13 September 1996).

– cannibalism. It was more than two months until the last few survivors were found and rescued.

━━━━━➤●◄━━━━━

PARANORMAL PLACES

There's no doubt that some places attract more than their fair share of unlikely occurrences – but surely it's just coincidence …?

The Town that Caught Tourette's

The small town of Le Roy, New York was nicknamed the Town that Caught Tourette's in 2012 after a documentary revealed that eighteen local teenage girls had inexplicably all developed the syndrome around the same time.

The bizarre coincidence – or epidemic – began when a sixteen-year-old cheerleader woke to find her chin jutting forward and her face spasming uncontrollably. The original diagnosis – an anxiety attack – was overruled when MRI scans showed that her facial contortions were in fact tics consistent with

Tourette's. Two weeks later, another cheerleader at the same school suffered an attack of even more extreme symptoms – stuttering and jerking – and before long almost twenty teens, many of them unknown to each other, had come forward with the same terrifying condition.

The cause of what doctors have termed 'mass psychogenic illness' remains unclear. While some fingers point to Le Roy's manufacturing past and the environmental toxins it may have left behind – one mother went so far as to call in Erin Brockovich, the environmental campaigner immortalized by Julia Roberts in a film of the same name – medical professionals have speculated as to whether the girls are simply dealing with the stresses and traumas of teenage life.

But all at the same time, in the same town? What are the odds of that?

Stonehenge

Stonehenge, the circle of prehistoric standing stones that has survived for up to 5,000 years on Salisbury Plain, England, has had countless meanings attached to it over the millennia, many of them eyebrow-raising in the extreme. One theory, set out by historian Geoffrey of Monmouth in the twelfth century, is that Stonehenge was built by the wizard Merlin, using stones brought to Salisbury by African giants. Another states that the vast stones were brought there by the Devil, who had purchased them from a woman in Ireland.

The monument's current association with modern-day paganism has done little to convince most people that any theories, however rational, can possibly be correct – but two of them stand out as being either spot on or incredibly coincidental. The first is the alignment of the sun during the summer solstice – 21 June – when it invariably rises between two of the outlying stones and shines straight through the entrance of Stonehenge and on to the altar. Given the primitive nature of scientific understanding in 3000 BC, this is nothing short of astounding.

The second theory, outlined by California scientist Steven Waller in 2012, is that the layout of Stonehenge matches an 'auditory illusion' that its builders may

have been aware of from their own musical rituals. Waller showed that when two identical instruments play the same note continuously, our ears in fact hear what sounds like waves of slightly louder and slightly quieter noise. To illustrate this, he attached two flutes to a pump in order to maintain a continuous note and then walked some blindfolded volunteers in a circle around the sound. They too reported hearing this auditory illusion – waves of volume – and said it was as if objects placed at regular intervals were getting in between them and the origin of the sound.

When Waller asked them to draw diagrams of these 'obstructions' they had experienced, a number of participants sketched what looked remarkably like the layout of Stonehenge ...

'If these people in the past were dancing in a circle around two pipers and were experiencing the loud and soft and loud and soft regions that happen when an interference pattern is set up, they would have felt there were these massive objects arranged in a ring,' he told the American Association for the Advancement of Science. 'I think that was what motivated them to build the actual structure that matched this virtual impression. It was like a vision that they received from the other world.'

HOW DID
THEY KNOW?

WHETHER or not you believe in the power of prophecy, it's always unnerving when predictions turn out to be true. Surely they're nothing but lucky guesses – right?

———>●<———

'Coincidence is God's way of
remaining anonymous.'

ALBERT EINSTEIN

———>●<———

NOSTRA-DAMNED-US

Michel de Nostredame, better known as Nostradamus, was a sixteenth-century French apothecary and reputed seer best known for his book *Les Prophéties* (*The Prophecies*), first published in 1555 and in print ever since. Generation after generation have appropriated Nostradamus's writings as truthful predictions of major events. Below are a few choice examples. Make of them what you will ...

———⟫●⟪———

PROPHESY:

'The blood of the just will be demanded of
London,
Burnt by the fire in the year 66.'

EVENT: THE GREAT FIRE OF LONDON IN 1666

This raging inferno destroyed the medieval City of London and is estimated to have burned the homes of 70,000 of the City's 80,000 inhabitants. The number of those who actually lost their lives is mercifully thought to be in single digits.

Prophesy:

'From the enslaved people, songs, chants and
    demands,
The princes and lords are held captive in prisons:
In the future by such headless idiots
These will be taken as divine utterances …
Before the war comes
The great wall will fall,
The King will be executed; his death, coming too
    soon, will be lamented.
[The guards] will swim in blood,
Near the River Seine the soil will be bloodied.'

Event: The French Revolution of 1789

This bloody rebellion saw aristocrats and royalty
arrested and beheaded by guillotine; the large,
central fortress-like prison, the Bastille, was
stormed and ultimately demolished; and the
captive King of France, Louis XVI, was executed
in 1793. The king's execution was four years after
the revolution started – so not quite 'too soon' –
but there's no telling that to Nostradamus's fan
club.

PROPHESY:

'From the depths of the West of Europe
A young child will be born of poor people,
He who by his tongue will seduce a great troop;
His fame will increase towards the realm of the
    East.'

EVENT: HITLER AND THE RISE OF NATIONAL SOCIALISM

Also referred to as 'the Germany child', the figure referred to here is invariably taken to be Adolf Hitler, fascist chancellor of Germany from 1933 to 1945 and progenitor of World War II and the Holocaust.

PROPHESY:

'Volcanic fire from the centre of the earth
Will cause trembling around the new city:
Two great rocks will make war for a long time.
Then Arethusa will redden a new river …'

EVENT: THE 9/11 ATTACK ON THE WORLD TRADE CENTER IN NEW YORK

Those keen to see the shadow of Nostradamus hovering over this tragic event read the 'centre of the earth' as its trade centre, the 'new city' as New York and the 'two great rocks' as the towers or alternatively the religions of Christianity and Islam. Other verses are falsely cited to back up the 9/11 claim, including references to 'steel birds' (the aeroplanes that crashed into the towers), wilfully ignoring the fact that steel wasn't invented until the nineteenth century.

One thing we do know is that Nostradamus foresaw his own death, albeit not in his usual cryptic manner. On his deathbed he reportedly said: 'Tomorrow, I shall no longer be here.' He was spot on.

⟹●⟸

PECULIAR PROPHECIES

From prophetic dreams to gut feelings, the world of coincidences would be a lesser place without what in psychoanalytical circles must surely be known as 'crazy hunches'.

⟫●⟪

The Legend Returns

The power of prophecy certainly worked in the favour of Spanish Conquistador Hernán Cortés when he was sent to conquer and claim Mexico in 1519. His arrival happily coincided with the year in the Mayan calendar when the man-god Quetzalcoatl was due to return to reclaim the city of Tenochtitlán. By all accounts the native Aztecs believed Cortés to be this legendary figure, who appears as a half-man, half-feathered serpent in Aztec artefacts – a mistake that assisted Cortés in capturing Mexico with relative ease. We can only assume the explorer wasn't much of a looker, given his apparent resemblance to a feathered snake.

Interestingly, some Mormons have co-opted Quetzalcoatl into their own mythology. In Aztec legend, the man-god came from the sky and promised to return, which to many Latter-Day Saints sounds

suspiciously like the career trajectory of Jesus Christ. No doubt Cortés would have found this comparison infinitely more flattering.

THE SKY IS FALLING!

In 2012 the world was gripped by an end-of-days paranoia of Chicken Licken proportions. Why? The Mesoamerican Long Count calendar, erroneously AKA the Mayan calendar, had been calculated as simply coming to an end on 21 December 2012, after which: who knew? On the assumption that the world was about to end, thousands of believers from Stonehenge to South America took part in commemorative events – while tens of thousands descended on the tiny French hamlet of Bugarach, whose mystical energy was due to ward off Armageddon – but it was all for nought. Perhaps the Mayans had simply run out of blank pages?

An Uninvited Guest

In the early 1960s a young woman suffering from depression decided to end it all by inhaling gas from her oven. She was already unconscious when there was a knock at the front door, which was then kicked in by a man who rushed to her aid and saved her life. The man was Douglas Johnson, a medium whom the young woman had consulted a number of years earlier. In a series of coincidences, he had got on the wrong bus, ended up outside the woman's building and decided to call on her unannounced. In a 1967 lecture to the Cambridge Society for Psychical Research, Johnson recalled that it was only when he got to her front door and smelled gas that he realized she was in danger.

⟫●⟪

PRESIDENTIAL PREMONITION I

After the assassination of Abraham Lincoln, his friend Ward Hill Lamon wrote a biography of the president, *Recollections of Abraham Lincoln 1847–1865*, in which he recounted an eerily prophetic nightmare Lincoln had had just three days before his death. In Lincoln's own words:

'There seemed to be a death-like stillness about me. Then I heard subdued sobs, as if a number of people were weeping. I thought I left my bed and wandered downstairs. There the silence was broken by the same pitiful sobbing, but the mourners were invisible …

Determined to find the cause of a state of things so mysterious and so shocking, I kept on until I arrived at the East Room, which I entered. There I met with a sickening surprise. Before me was a catafalque, on which rested a corpse wrapped in funeral vestments. Around it were stationed soldiers who were acting as guards; and there was a throng of people, gazing mournfully upon the corpse, whose face was covered, others weeping pitifully. "Who is dead in the White House?" I demanded of one of the soldiers. "The President," was his answer; "He was killed by an assassin." Then came a loud burst of grief from the crowd, which woke me from my dream.'

THE PRINTED WORD

It's all very well saying, after the fact, that you knew something was going to happen – but if the evidence is there for all to see in cold, hard print, it's almost impossible for anyone to remain sceptical.

PRESIDENTIAL PREMONITION II

Given the string of weird coincidences linking the assassinations of Presidents Lincoln and Kennedy (see p.60), it should come as no surprise that JFK also prophesied his own death just hours before it happened.

On the morning of 22 November 1963, Jackie Kennedy was unnerved by a full-page ad placed in the *Dallas Morning News* – not so much because it accused the president of being a Communist sympathizer but rather because it had a black border and resembled a death notice. JFK tried to comfort her with the words: 'We're heading into nut country today. But, Jackie, if somebody wants to shoot me from a window with a rifle, nobody can stop it, so why worry about it?'

That Kennedy made such a comment about his own assassination on the day he was shot is coincidence enough, but that he so casually predicted the precise method of his death is nothing short of sinister.

———➤●◄———

'I always avoid prophesying beforehand, because it is a much better policy to prophesy after the event has already taken place.'

WINSTON CHURCHILL

———➤●◄———

WHOLE LOTTO LUCK

When the *Columbian* newspaper in Washington State accidentally printed the wrong lottery numbers from the previous evening's Pick 4 Oregon Lottery in June 2000, editors were surprised the error warranted a visit from detectives. It transpired that they had mistakenly printed Virginia's winning numbers from the previous evening – which were identical to the numbers drawn in Oregon the day after the newspaper was circulated.

Despite the minuscule odds, lottery coincidences do happen. In New Jersey in 1986, one woman won the state lottery twice in four months. In Bulgaria in September 2009, the same six numbers won two consecutive draws. Suspicions were raised when it was revealed that there were eighteen winners in the second draw, versus none for the first, but officials could find no explanation other than coincidence.

'I wager this combination will be played in the Bulgarian lottery for a very long time,' UCLA professor of statistics Don Ylvisaker told the *Wall Street Journal*.

<hr />

THE WRITING ON THE WALL

The most terrifying thing about 1982's *Poltergeist* is not the ghosts, the creepy little girl or the things that go bang in the night. Rather, it is a bizarre blink-and-you'll-miss-it prophecy contained in the background scenery.

In the scene in which a clown toy comes to life in little Robbie's bedroom, a Super Bowl poster can be seen on the wall behind his bed. It is eerie enough that the poster advertises Super Bowl XXII – a fixture that didn't take place until six years after the film's release – but eerier still that the date of this game, 31 January 1988, is when the franchise's child star, Heather O'Rourke, became violently unwell and subsequently died.

———————

BEHOLD THE FRONT PAGE

In March 1977, a student at Duke University, North Carolina, astounded his peers and professors by demonstrating an eerie knack for prediction live on television.

Lee Fried, an amateur magician who took his inspiration from the great Harry Houdini, wrote out two predictions about the following day's newspaper headlines, sealed them in an envelope and locked it in the university president's desk drawer, all under the watchful eye of the president himself. The following morning the envelope was opened in front of cameras at a local TV station.

Fried's first prediction was about a basketball game between the University of North Carolina and Marquette University; the headline he had foreseen was 'Marquette Bursts UNC Bubble; Wins 68–58'. The actual headline read 'Marquette Pokes Hole in Tar Heels Bubble' and the score was 67–59. His fellow students were moderately impressed.

But even cynics were won over to Fried's supernatural skills when he revealed his predicted headline for the *News and Observer*'s front page: '583 Die in Collision of 747s in Worst Disaster in Aviation History'. The actual headline read '530 Killed as Jets Collide in Fog: Worst Air Disaster in History', with the death toll subsequently confirmed as 583.

'The human mind is shrouded in mystery' was Fried's enigmatic conclusion.

━━━⇒➤●◄⇐━━━

CONSPIRACY OR COINCIDENCE?

WORLD-FAMOUS coincidences – especially those even vaguely connected to politics – have a tendency to veer into the realm of conspiracy theories. *How convenient*, people say to themselves, *that this unlikely series of events should have occurred as and when it did. Didn't that work out well for the government/the war/our alien overlords?* Make of these stories what you will – but beware of who might secretly be monitoring your reaction as you read them ...

'We have learned in recent years to
translate almost all of political life in
terms of conspiracy.'

JOHN LE CARRÉ

———⟫●⟪———

WEIRD HISTORY

Increasingly, the dust has barely settled after an
important world event before whispers of conspiracy
begin to be heard. Soon the craziest of claims
becomes common knowledge and before long
public commentary falls into two categories: entirely
convinced of an audacious cover-up or entirely
sceptical (but quietly curious). Here are just three
examples of world events that have taken on a bizarre
alternate narrative.

———⟫●⟪———

The Roswell Incident

'RAAF [Roswell Army Air Field] Captures Flying Saucer on Ranch in Roswell Region' announced the headline of the *Roswell Daily Record* on 8 July 1947, forever damning the New Mexico town to speculation that alien life forms roam among the population and that the so-called 'flying saucer' continues to lie hidden somewhere in its midst.

A press released issued by the RAAF that same day – the source for the newspaper story – stated that 'The many rumors regarding the flying disc became a reality yesterday when the intelligence office of ... Roswell Army Air Field was fortunate enough to gain possession of a disc through the cooperation of one of the local ranchers ... The flying object landed on a ranch near Roswell sometime last week ... It was inspected at the Roswell Army Air Field and subsequently loaned by Major Marcel to higher headquarters.' The local rancher in question was William Brazel, who had stumbled across a 'large area of bright wreckage made up of rubber strips, tinfoil, a rather tough paper and sticks'. His discovery was sent to Fort Worth Army Air Field in Texas for further analysis.

By the next morning, 9 July, with the nation's press in a frenzy about the flying saucer, the army had issued

a statement revealing, as the *Los Angeles Times* put it, 'Grounded Flying Saucer Only a Weather Balloon'. Unsurprisingly, this did little to assuage the suspicions of conspiracy theorists. Was it really conceivable that, by some fluke, everybody at the RAAF was so unfamiliar with this standard piece of meteorological equipment that they not only called it a 'flying object' and sent it away for examination, but also felt compelled to contact the press?

A new admission by the United States Air Force in 1994, that the 'weather balloon' had in fact been a radar device secretly picking up transmissions from Russia, added fuel to the fire, as did its claim in 1997 that reports of supposed 'alien sightings' were the result of people misremembering an army experiment in which adult-sized dummies had been thrown from aircraft over Roswell – especially since this experiment took place ten years after the Roswell Incident.

———⇒●⇐———

The Moon Landings

On 20 July 1969 Apollo 11 took three American astronauts to the moon, where two of them – Neil Armstrong and Buzz Aldrin – spent a couple of hours bouncing around and collecting lunar matter. Or did they?

The (supposed) Moon Landings have divided public opinion for almost five decades, with loud voices on either side insisting that they obviously were or were not faked. Was it all a vast conspiracy or is the cynics' 'evidence' just a series of convenient coincidences? Here are just a few of the most popular pros and cons.

Conspiracy: The photos are too good and must have been taken in a studio.

Coincidence: NASA only published the best ones.

Conspiracy: Shadows on the moon seem to fall in different directions, indicating the use of studio lights.

Coincidence: With light coming from the Sun, from the module and, in reflection, from Earth, and then being diffused by lunar dust and captured by wide-angled camera lenses, this is to be expected.

Conspiracy: The photos show no stars, and when questioned the astronauts had no recollection of seeing stars.

Coincidence: It was lunar daytime when Apollo 11 landed. The light of the Sun made the stars invisible to the naked eye.

Conspiracy: The background looks identical in most of the photos.

Coincidence: It's the moon. There's not much to see.

Conspiracy: Who on earth was filming Neil Armstrong as he became the 'first' man to step onto the moon?

Coincidence: The camera was built into the side of the Lunar Module and could be popped out as and when needed.

Conspiracy: The American flag was clearly fluttering in a non-existent breeze.

Coincidence: An illusion: the flag was simply crumpled from having been folded.

Conspiracy: All six manned landings occurred under President Richard Nixon. Surely advances in technology have made successful moon landings more rather than less likely over the past five decades?

Coincidence: What nation or political leader would fork out billions just to be second best?

'People love conspiracy theories.'

NEIL ARMSTRONG

———>➤●≪<———

> Doing little to dispel theories that the Moon Landings were an elaborate practical joke is this anagram of Neil Armstrong's famous one-liner, devised by Steve Krakowski. The letters of *'That's one small step for a man; one giant leap for mankind.' Neil A. Armstrong*, when scrambled, make: 'A thin man ran, makes a large stride, left planet, pins flag on moon … on to Mars!'

9/11

No event in history has generated as many conspiracy theories as 9/11. The theories cover every permutation and variously involve hologram-wrapped missiles made to look like planes, the controlled demolition of the Twin Towers, and major government cover-ups of every possible variety.

On 11 September 2002, one year after the terrorist attacks on the United States, the winning numbers in one of New York's lottery picks were 9-1-1.

But one strand of conspiratorial thinking has proven quite eerie, and that is the extraordinary number of elevens associated with the attacks. There are eleven letters in 'New York City', 'The Pentagon', 'George W. Bush' and 'Afghanistan'. New York was the eleventh state admitted to the union. American Airlines Flight 11 was the first plane to hit the Twin Towers, which incidentally looked like a giant 11, with 92 people aboard; 9 + 2 = 11. United Airlines Flight 175, which struck the South Tower, was carrying 65 people; 6 + 5 = 11. Meanwhile, 11 September is the 254th day of the year (2 + 5 + 4 = 11), with 111 days remaining. Even the popular rendering of the date – 9/11 – adds up to eleven (9 + 1 + 1), as well as resembling the US emergency number, 911.

Coincidence? It gets weirder. On 11 March 2004, ten coordinated explosions on four packed commuter trains killed 191 people in Madrid. Numerologists were quick to point out that the date not only contained another eleven and added up to eleven (1 + 1 + 3 + 2 + 0 + 0 + 4 = 11), as did the number of victims (1 + 9 + 1 = 11), but also that it fell exactly 911 days after 9/11. This last part isn't quite right – thanks to 2004 being a leap year the two attacks were 912 days apart – but it would be accurate to say there were 911 clear days between the two dates.

———⟫●⟪———

'When coincidences pile up in this way, one cannot help being impressed by them – for the greater the number of terms in such a series, or the more unusual its character, the more improbable it becomes.'

CARL JUNG

———⟫●⟪———

POLITICAL PARANOIA

'If voting changed anything,' early-twentieth-century anarchist Emma Goldman said, 'they'd make it illegal.' Is there, as some suspect, a secret conspiracy that propels certain people to power and then influences their policies once there? If these stories are anything to go by: probably, yes.

The End is Nigh

In 1942, at the height of World War II, civilians on both sides of the Atlantic were filled with joy when newspapers ran notices suggesting that a secret code between world leaders indicated the imminent end of hostilities. Entitled 'An Interesting Look at World Leaders in 1942', the notices generally looked something like Table A on the opposite page.

For many people, hopeful of an end to the misery of war, this alignment of coincidences seemed too good to be true – as of course it was. Indeed, by tweaking the maths, newspapers were able to print much the same thing two years later, entitled 'What

Table A

	Churchill	Hitler	Roosevelt	Il Duce	Stalin	Tojo
Born	1874	1889	1882	1883	1879	1884
Age in 1942	68	53	60	59	63	58
Years in Office	2	9	9	20	18	1
Took Office	1940	1933	1933	1922	1924	1941
TOTAL	3884	3884	3884	3884	3884	3884

One-half of 3884 = 1942   First letter of each man's name = C-H-R-I-S-T

Table B

	Churchill	Hitler	Roosevelt	Il Duce	Stalin	Tojo
Born	1874	1889	1882	1883	1879	1884
Took Office	1940	1933	1933	1922	1924	1941
Age in 1944	70	55	62	61	65	60
Years in Office	4	11	11	22	20	3
TOTAL	3886	3886	3886	3886	3886	3886

END OF WAR: ½ of 3886 equals 1944, ½ of 1944 equals September 7th at 2 o'clock.

To find Supreme Ruler, take the first letter of the above names. CHRIST

Do You Think of This?', in order to prove that 1944 was preordained to be the year of victory (*See* Table B on the previous page).

Alas, the supposed conspiracy still failed to achieve peace and the war went on for yet another year.

━━━━━━►●◄━━━━━━

SINISTER?

There are numerous similarities between history's great political leaders that wouldn't raise an eyebrow; it is no great coincidence, for example, that nineteen British Prime Ministers have been educated at Eton and twenty-six of them went to Oxford. But over in the United States, eagle-eyed political pundits have noticed an unusual trend among presidents: an inordinate number of them have been left-handed.

In a country where only 10 per cent of the population is left-handed, 50 per cent of post-war presidents have been left-handed – indeed, five of the last seven presidents have been. In the 2008 election both candidates were left-handed, while in 1992 and 1996 all three of them were.

A conspiracy of the left-handed or just a highly improbable coincidence?

———>●<———

HINDSIGHT IS TWENTY-TWENTY

While right-handed politicians may as well give up any ambition of becoming president of the United States, it seems politicians of either handedness do well to avoid seeking public office in years divisible by twenty. Since 1840, every president elected in a year divisible by twenty has died – by fair means or foul – during his term in office.

William Henry Harrison died of pneumonia shortly after his election in 1840. Abraham Lincoln (1860) was assassinated during his second term and both James A. Garfield (1880) and William McKinley (1900) were shot a year after successful elections. Warren G. Harding (1920) and Franklin D. Roosevelt (1940) both died of natural causes while in office, and John F. Kennedy (1960) was assassinated.

The two exceptions to this particular curse are Ronald Reagan (1980), just – he was shot during his first term but the bullet missed his heart by an inch – and George W. Bush (2000), who somehow survived his two terms unscathed.

CURIOUSER AND CURIOUSER

Aliens, monsters, futuristic warfare: all under our very noses, if only we could read the coincidences correctly ...

No Word of a Lie

Alien abductions went through something of a heyday in the wake of the Roswell Incident (see p.146), especially in the United States, but by far the most difficult case for sceptics to dismiss was that of Travis Walton, an Arizona logger who disappeared for five whole days in November 1975 after apparently being zapped by a spaceship.

That evening, Walton and the six men on his team saw a bright light and approached what turned out to be a hovering disc. Walton walked towards it and was struck, apparently fatally, by a beam of light; his co-workers escaped in their vehicle. When they later returned, there was no sign of Walton or the UFO.

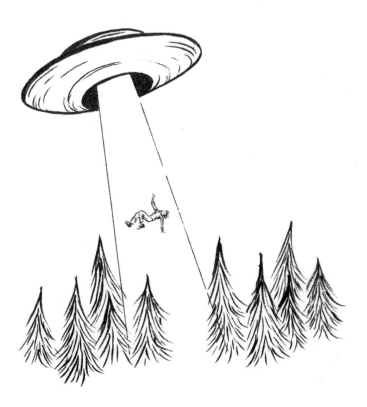

In the five days during which Walton was missing, the six loggers were subjected to lie-detector tests by the Arizona Department of Public Safety. The report sent to the investigating sheriff concluded that at least five of the six men 'were being truthful' in their account and they 'did see some object that they believe to be a UFO … If an actual UFO did not exist and the UFO is a man-made hoax, five of these men had no prior knowledge of a hoax.'

Travis Walton reappeared in a neighbouring town on 10 November, visibly shaken and visibly thinner, with a detailed account of his five days at the hands of short, bald, huge-eyed figures aboard the UFO. He too passed a lie-detector test, although he also failed at least one.

━━━⟫●⟪━━━

DOOMED DATE

Conspiracy fans were intrigued in 2009 to hear that Michael Jackson's star-studded memorial service would be held on 7 July – exactly seven years to the day since he signed his will.

GIVE US A CLUE

In the spring of 1944, with World War II entering its decisive stages, the Allied powers found themselves rather unusually preoccupied with the *Daily Telegraph*'s cryptic crossword puzzles. The reason was that the solutions had begun corresponding with secret D-Day codewords.

At first, the appearance of Juno, Gold and Sword – codenames for three of the D-Day landing beaches – seemed coincidental. But suspicions were raised at MI5 in May 1944 when the solutions included not only Utah and Omaha – the other two landing beaches – but also Mulberry (the code for floating harbours), Neptune (the naval assault phase) and, most alarmingly, Overlord, the codename for the whole D-Day campaign.

The crossword compiler, headmaster Leonard Dawe, was interrogated on suspicion of espionage, but he was adamant that the solutions were nothing more than a fluke – something with which he was familiar, having been interrogated two years earlier when his crossword solution Dieppe coincidentally appeared on the morning of the failed raid on Dieppe.

It was not until 1984 that the full story of the D-Day crosswords began to emerge. Ronald French, a former pupil of Dawe's, revealed that he and a number of other boys had helped the headmaster compile his crosswords, suggesting words for which Dawe would then write a cryptic clue. In the spring of 1944, French had encountered a camp of American and Canadian troops near the school grounds and had taken to playing truant in order to visit them, and it was here that he overheard the D-Day codewords that found their way into the *Daily Telegraph*.

'I was totally obsessed about the whole thing,' he recalled. 'Hundreds of kids must have known what I knew.'

Monster Madness

In 1975, at the height of the Loch Ness Monster craze, eminent British conservationist Sir Peter Scott gave the alleged creature a scientific name so that it could be listed as an endangered species. He chose *Nessiteras rhombopteryx*, 'Ness monster with a diamond-shaped fin', based on a couple of blurry underwater photographs.

The validity of Scott's work on the Loch Ness Monster was undermined somewhat when Scottish politician Nicholas Fairbairn rearranged the letters of *Nessiteras rhombopteryx* to create 'Monster hoax by Sir Peter S', although another Nessie fan, Robert H. Rines, re-scrambled the letters to come up with a retort against the cynics: 'Yes, both pix are monsters, R.'

LITERAL
LITERATURE

THE brains behind some of our greatest literary works are no strangers to happenstance. From celebrated writers who've predicted their own deaths to authors encountering their doppelgänger, via the eerie propensity for fiction to become fact, the literary world is packed full of examples of coincidence.

———➤●◄———

'Coincidences are spiritual puns.'

G.K. CHESTERTON

STRANGER THAN FICTION

Novelists are, by definition, inventors. They conceive unlikely scenarios to befall imaginary people whose names are plucked from thin air. So how come so many fictional tales go on to be played out in reality?

Poe, Pym and Parker

Edgar Allan Poe, the nineteenth-century author known for his macabre tales, wrote one novel during his illustrious career. *The Narrative of Arthur Gordon Pym of Nantucket* (1838) is a series of fabulous and sometimes near-fatal adventures, including an account of the fictional shipwreck *Grampus*. When the whaling ship capsizes, Richard Parker, one of four surviving sailors set adrift, suggests that the starving men draw lots to decide which of them should be sacrificed and eaten by the others – a plan that backfires and results in him being cannibalized.

This disquieting anecdote was mirrored in real life some years later in 1884, when the yacht *Mignonette* sank, leaving four survivors adrift in a lifeboat. When the hunger became too much, one of them, a cabin boy, was killed and eaten by the others. His name was Richard Parker.

———⟫●⟪———

> 'Any coincidence,' said Miss Marple to herself, 'is always worth noting. You can throw it away later if it is only a coincidence.'
>
> AGATHA CHRISTIE, *NEMESIS*

———⟫●⟪———

WHAT IF?

In one of the eeriest literary coincidences of recent times, British author Chris Cleave's debut novel, *Incendiary*, about an al-Qaeda attack on London, was published on 7 July 2005 – the date of al-Qaeda's devastating attack on the London transport system.

The timing was unbelievable. In the days preceding the book's launch, the author later recalled on his website 'hundreds of posters went up on the London Underground featuring the smoking London skyline and the headline: "WHAT IF?"' In the aftermath, book chain Waterstones felt compelled to cancel the advertising it had planned.

Fortunately for Cleave, the book's merit ultimately shone through. It has been published in over twenty countries, won numerous prizes and been made into a film starring Ewan McGregor and Michelle Williams.

―――――>⊙<―――――

ALL AT SEA

Former Prime Minister Edward Heath must have thought he was having a nightmare when he learned, on 4 September 1974, that his yacht *Morning Cloud III* had been lost at sea en route to the Isle of Wight, just two days after a similar fate had befallen his former yacht *Morning Cloud I*. The previous week he had posed for a photo with author John Dyson at the launch of his thriller *The Prime Minister's Boat is Missing*.

'Nothing is as obnoxious as other
people's luck.'

F. SCOTT FITZGERALD

By the Book

When, in 1974, American newspaper heiress Patty
Hearst was kidnapped by shadowy revolutionaries
calling themselves the Symbionese Liberation Army,
subsequently appearing in taped recordings to denounce
her wealthy parents and declare her support for her
captors, the FBI had plenty to contend with. But by
far their most pressing questions were reserved for an
unknown author named Harrison James, who two
years earlier had published a novel that essentially – and
apparently coincidentally – outlined the details of the
Patty Hearst case.

In *Black Abductor*, a violent and pornographic
tale that was tastefully reissued as *Abduction: Fiction
Before Fact* in the wake of the real-life kidnapping,
a wealthy heiress named Patricia is taken hostage
by shadowy revolutionaries whose cause she soon

begins publically endorsing. Both girls were snatched in the presence of their boyfriends, who were doubly unfortunate in being both badly beaten and originally suspected of masterminding the crime, and both cases were brought to a successful and very high-profile conclusion, with arrests all round for the captors and redemption for the errant teens.

LOST IN A NOVEL

The American novelist and essayist Ambrose Bierce built a formidable literary career on tales of dark, surreal and chilling occurrences. In October 1913, at the age of seventy-one, he travelled alone to Mexico via a number of Civil War battlegrounds – and was never seen again.

George v. George

George Orwell's *Nineteen Eighty-Four* (1949), supposedly a dystopian satire, has given us many things, from the TV show *Big Brother* to terms such as 'Newspeak'. But in the decade following 9/11, it suddenly looked as if Orwell had predicted the fate of the modern world alarmingly accurately.

The connection between 'Big Brother is watching' and our world of CCTV, biometric scanning and 'enhanced interrogation' is easy to make. But critics of George W. Bush in particular have also compared Oceania's state of perpetual but nebulous war in *Nineteen Eighty-Four* with the war waged by the United States and its allies against a specific Saudi Arabian terrorist, then Afghanistan, then the 'Axis of Evil', and then a major campaign in Iraq while simultaneously sizing up Iran.

Perhaps giving political commentators greatest cause for concern, however, was the ease with which Bush's notorious verbal gaffes veered into Big Brother territory. 'War is Peace,' the Ministry of Truth insists in *Nineteen Eighty-Four*; 'I just want you to know,' Bush said in June 2002, 'that, when we talk about war, we're really talking about peace.'

'Amid the action and reaction of so dense a swarm of humanity, every possible combination of events may be expected to take place, and many a little problem will be presented which may be striking and bizarre.'

ARTHUR CONAN DOYLE,
THE ADVENTURE OF THE BLUE CARBUNCLE

———❯●❮———

UNSINKABLE, AGAIN

We all know the story of the 'unsinkable' British luxury liner that set off at unprecedented speed across the Atlantic one April over a century ago, with a woefully small number of lifeboats aboard, and which tragically sank after hitting an iceberg, with the loss of more than half its passengers.

Author Morgan Robertson certainly knew the story – he wrote it – and must have been unnerved when he heard of the demise of the *Titanic* on 15 April 1912. Fourteen years earlier, in 1898, he had published his novel *Futility, or the Wreck of the Titan*, in which a liner named *Titan* sinks in eerily similar circumstances to the doomed *Titanic*.

I Spy

Norman Mailer's *Barbary Shore* (1951), a tale of espionage and intrigue in Brooklyn, unfortunately fulfilled the stereotype of the 'difficult second novel' and was universally panned – but the sinister story that emerged after it was published is far more intriguing ...

The novel's protagonist is an author who holes himself up in a Brooklyn boarding house to write a novel, little suspecting that one of his neighbours might be a Russian spy. It was only in 1957, when the FBI and US Immigration Service swooped on Mailer's own Brooklyn writing studio, that he discovered the man in the studio beneath him was none other than

Vilyam Genrikhovich Fisher, AKA Rudolf Abel, a KGB agent under deep cover.

'I am sure we used to be in the elevator together many times,' Mailer later said. 'It made me decide that there's no clear boundary between experience and imagination. Who knows what glimpses of reality we pick up unconsciously, telepathically.'

<hr />

SPACE RACE

Jules Verne is best known for his novels about circumnavigating the earth or indeed travelling to the centre of it, but in one of his rare fictional journeys into space he unwittingly predicted a disaster that would occur over a century later.

Around the Moon (1870) tells of a near-catastrophic space mission aboard the *Columbiad*; unable to land on the moon due to an oxygen explosion, the astronauts have to reroute to the far side of the moon in order to be propelled back to earth by gravitational pull. They crash-land in the Pacific and are rescued by boat. In April 1995 the Apollo 13 space mission

– launched at 13.13, auspiciously enough – ran into almost identical difficulties when an oxygen tank exploded; the crew had to reroute to the far side of the moon in order to be propelled back to earth by gravitational pull. They crash-landed in the Pacific and were rescued by boat.

⎯⎯►●◄⎯⎯

SOLE SURVIVOR

In the 7 September 1905 edition of London newspaper *The Graphic*, in response to a previous article about coincidences, the following note from British playwright Arthur Law appeared in the 'Letters to the Editor' section:

'Sir – Among many strange coincidences which I have experienced in my time, one of the most singular which I can recall at the moment happened to me in connection with a play which I wrote some twenty years ago for the German Reed entertainment. One of my characters was named Robert Golding, and for the requirements of the plot I had made him the sole survivor of the crew of a ship called the *Caroline*, which had been lost at sea. A few days after the production of the play I read in a newspaper an account of the shipwreck of a vessel named the *Caroline*, which had gone down with all hands, with one exception, and this exception was a man of the name of Golding. Now Golding is not at all a common name, and the circumstance of his being, both in fact and fiction, the sole survivor of the shipwrecked *Caroline*, impressed me at the time as being a coincidence of a very peculiar nature.

'Yours faithfully, Arthur Law.'

———————⇒➤●◄⇐———————

YOU COULDN'T MAKE IT UP

Authors are of course known for spinning tall tales and spellbinding mysteries that keep us gripped and entertained. But every now and then the mirror is turned, and it is the authors themselves who become the subject of bizarre and uncanny stories.

———————⇒➤●◄⇐———————

THE END IS NIGH

The American writer Mark Twain was born on the day of the appearance of Halley's Comet in 1835. In 1909, the year before his death, he was reported to have said: 'I came in with Halley's Comet in 1835. It is coming again next year, and I expect to go out with it. It will be the greatest disappointment of my life if I don't go out with Halley's Comet. The Almighty has said, no doubt, "Now here are these two unaccountable freaks; they came in together, they must go out together."'

Twain's wish was fulfilled: he died of a heart attack on 21 April 1910 in Redding, Connecticut, one day after the comet's closest approach to earth.

DOUBLE TROUBLE

In 1979 the German equivalent of *Reader's Digest*, *Das Beste*, invited readers to send in strange but true stories from their own lives. The winner was a Walter Kellner from Munich, who related the story of a doomed flight he made from Sardinia to Sicily in a Cessna 421. His engine malfunctioned and he was forced to crash-land.

When the story was published in the magazine, however, editors received an angry letter from another Walter Kellner – this one from Austria – who claimed that the competition winner had plagiarized his story and stolen his name. He insisted that it was he who had crash-landed a Cessna 421 between Sicily and Sardinia.

When the two men's tales were investigated further, it turned out that both were true.

———◆———

'To lose one parent, Mr Worthing,
may be regarded as a misfortune. To
lose both looks like carelessness.'

OSCAR WILDE,
THE IMPORTANCE OF BEING EARNEST

Date Fate

When author J. K. Rowling needed to choose a birth date for Harry Potter, it seemed natural enough that she would use her own birthday, 31 July. It was only many years later, when she was tracing her maternal ancestry at a records office in Paris, that she discovered that the grandfather she had never known had also been born on 31 July.

DA VINCI DECODED

Dan Brown's novel *The Da Vinci Code*, published in 2003 to frenzied scenes in bookshops the world over, pointed at an unprecedented level of conspiracy and cover-up around the life and legacy of Jesus Christ. Unprecedented, that is, until a number of claimants came forward alleging that they had indeed seen many elements of *The Da Vinci Code* before – in their own books.

The greatest challenge came from Michael Baigent and Richard Leigh, two of the three co-authors of *The Holy Blood and the Holy Grail* (1982), a historical hypothesis for the continuation of Jesus's bloodline into the present day amid, as above, an unprecedented level of conspiracy and cover-up. When their case against Brown was brought to court in 2005, Baigent and Leigh argued that *The Da Vinci Code* was not only a blatant novelization of their research, but also that Brown had left a number of clues in the text to prove it – notably the character Leigh Teabing (Teabing is an anagram of Baigent), who walks with a pronounced limp, just like their other co-author Henry Lincoln. Brown claimed that this last point at the very least was just a coincidence.

Perhaps surprisingly, the case was overturned in the High Court, the judge decreeing that a novelist must be free to use works of supposed non-fiction as the basis for his fiction. But in a happy coincidence for Baigent, Leigh and Lincoln, sales of their twenty-five-year-old book went through the roof.

<hr>

BACK TO THE FUTURE

Johann Wolfgang von Goethe, the nineteenth-century German poet and dramatist, claimed that while riding on the road to Drusenheim in north-eastern France, he encountered a sort of doppelgänger. Goethe said that he passed the man on the road, riding in the other direction, and the resemblance was uncanny, except that the other gent was wearing a grey suit with a gold trim, an outfit Goethe had never himself worn.

Eight years later Goethe was once again travelling on the same road, but in the opposite direction, when a bout of déjà vu reminded him of the earlier occurrence and he noted with puzzlement that he was wearing a grey suit trimmed with gold – the very match of the garb he'd seen eight years earlier.

Type, My Pretties

It has been claimed that an infinite number of monkeys at an infinite number of typewriters would surely, given enough time, bash out the complete works of William Shakespeare as part of their random output. It's an interesting theory that, happily for animal rights activists, remains unproven. But over the centuries a number of (human) researchers have found hidden messages behind some of the Bard's most famous lines.

Take, for instance, Hamlet's iconic soliloquy from the play of the same name: 'To be, or not to be: that is the question:/ Whether 'tis nobler in the mind to suffer/ The slings and arrows of outrageous fortune ...' In 1996 a student named Cory Calhoun reshuffled these letters to create a handy précis of Hamlet's words: 'In one of the Bard's best-thought-of tragedies, our insistent hero, Hamlet, queries on two fronts about how life turns rotten.'

Coincidence? It doesn't end there. By adding a few lines to the original Shakespeare – 'To be, or not to be: that is the question:/ Whether 'tis nobler in the mind to suffer/ The slings and arrows of outrageous fortune,/ Or to take arms against a sea of troubles/ And by opposing, end them' – and then mixing the letters up, other literary puzzlers have come up with either a literary critique: 'Is a befitting quote from one of Shakespeare's greatest tragedies. But why won't Hamlet's inspiring motto toss our stubborn hero's tortuous battle for life, on one hand, and death, on another?' – or a *Da Vinci Code*-style clue as to who really wrote the great Bard's works: 'I wrote all of that Shakespeare's plays, and the wife and I got together, did most of his sonnets for our entertainment. But tormentors oft attribute our brash quotes as being bogus. O! no! no! no!'

Is the whole of Shakespeare a front for a series of secret codes? Perhaps we should set an infinite number of monkeys the task of working it out.

———◦———

THE LAST PLACE
YOU LOOKED

To this day, the sum of my physics knowledge after five years of weekly lessons is one great fact on the subject of black holes: surely, our teacher told us, the only explanation is that they are filled with all the socks that go missing in the wash. Similarly, the Royal Mint estimates that the value of all the 1p coins lost down the back of British sofas is an incredible £65 million. But occasionally – very occasionally – objects that have been written off as irretrievably lost do show up again, and often in the unlikeliest of places ...

'Shallow men believe in luck. Strong men believe in cause and effect.'

RALPH WALDO EMERSON

PRICELESS POSSESSIONS

When you lose something that quite literally can't be replaced, you had better hope there's a happy coincidence waiting just around the corner ...

MARITIME MATRIMONY

When New South Wales snorkelling fanatic Nick Deeks lost his wedding ring beneath the waves at Nelson Bay, he knew there was little chance of finding it again. Nevertheless he returned the next day and scoured the ocean floor, and sure enough he found a ring. But it wasn't his.

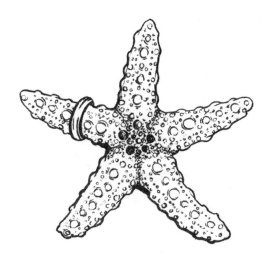

Deeks pocketed the ring and kept looking, and before long he was amazed to find his own. But how to reunite the first ring with its rightful owner? He made enquiries with locals and was directed to a nearby dive shop, whose owner still had a series of frantic emails in his inbox from British honeymooner Graeme Cappi, who had lost his wedding ring fifteen months earlier.

'He is gobsmacked at it being found,' said one of the local sleuths.

MATCHBOX MUDDLE

In an extraordinary double coincidence, two identical golden matchboxes that had been passed from hand to hand for twenty years were finally rediscovered on the same day.

In 1901 the Prince of Wales, later Edward VII, presented his actor friend Edward H. Sothern with a golden matchbox. Sothern attached it to a chain and wore it every day, but before long it had snapped loose in a foxhunting accident and been trampled underfoot. Embarrassed at having lost a gift from such an illustrious person, Sothern had an identical replacement made. The duplicate matchbox was in the possession of Sothern's son Sam, also an actor, when he travelled to Australia, and he gave it to a friend of his, Mr Labertouche, as thanks for his assistance during the trip.

In 1921, back in England, Sam was enjoying a day's foxhunting on the same land where the original had fallen into the mud. By some chance he got talking to an old farmhand who remembered Sothern Sr's accident and the subsequent loss of the first golden matchbox – which, funnily enough, he said, had been found again just that morning while the field was being ploughed.

Sothern Sr had died by now but Sam sent word of the bizarre coincidence to his brother, Edward, another actor, who was working in America at the time. On a cross-country train Edward read the letter out loud to his travelling companion, an Australian actor named Arthur Lawrence, who looked more and more astonished as the narrative unravelled. Lawrence then produced the original golden matchbox from his pocket. It had been a going-away gift from Mr Labertouche.

———⇒●⇐———

24-Carrot Gold

Christmas 1995 was somewhat ruined in the Paahlsson household of Mora, Sweden, when Mrs Paahlson realized she had lost her wedding ring during a busy day of cooking. She was so distressed that the whole family had to help tear up the kitchen flooring as part of the search, but it was all to no avail.

Sixteen years later, in 2011, Mrs Paahlson was digging for vegetables in her garden when she made an astonishing discovery: a carrot that was wedged into her wedding ring.

'The carrot was sprouting in the middle of the ring,' her husband told Swedish newspaper *Dagens Nyheter*. 'It's quite incredible.'

It would seem that the ring had been swept up with the vegetable peelings on that fateful Christmas Eve, and subsequently used as compost.

ONE CARELESS OWNER

A secretary from Berkshire was distraught after accidentally flushing an antique bracelet down the loo one morning in 1975. A number of months later Barbara Hutton was browsing for a replacement in a jewellery shop when a man came in asking for a valuation on a bracelet he had found while working in the sewer. Barbara recognized it as her own and it was returned – presumably after a good scrub – to its rightful place on her wrist.

'The man couldn't have known the bracelet belonged to me,' she told reporters. 'That he should be in the same shop on the same day is just fantastic.'

Fish Fingers

In June 2012, Haans Galassi of Washington State had a holiday to remember – for all the wrong reasons – when he went camping at Priest Lake, Idaho, and lost four of his fingers in a hideous wakeboarding accident.

But the story took on a bizarre new twist in September of that year when he received a phone call from an Idaho sheriff.

'He said that a fisherman was out on Priest Lake and I pretty much knew exactly what he was going to say at that point,' Galassi later recalled. 'I was like, "Let me guess, they found my fingers in a fish."'

Remarkably, that is indeed what had happened: angler Nolan Colvin had caught a trout in the lake and was cleaning the fish when he discovered the stub of a finger in its stomach.

Galassi declined the sheriff's offer of a reunion with his semi-digested former digit.

WHERE DID YOU LAST SEE IT?

Had anyone in the history of the world ever been able to answer this unhelpful question, the notion of 'lost property' would surely be obsolete.

⟹●⟸

THAT'S MY BABY

On the eve of World War I, a German woman photographed her young son and took the film plate to a Strasbourg shop for development. In the turmoil of the war she forgot to collect the photo and had to leave the city. Two years later, now living in Frankfurt, she took another film plate in for development, this time a picture of her new daughter. When she saw the photograph she was amazed: thanks to a double exposure, the picture of her daughter was superimposed onto the 'lost' picture of her son. Somehow the Strasbourg film plate had been not only mislabelled as unused and sent to Frankfurt, but then also bought by the woman who technically owned it already.

'Diligence is the mother of good luck.'

BENJAMIN FRANKLIN

———➤●◄———

SWITCHING ROOMS

In 1953, Chicago news reporter Irv Kupcinet was staying at London's Savoy Hotel while covering the coronation of Queen Elizabeth II. He was surprised to find someone else's belongings in one of the drawers, but astonished when he realized they belonged to his friend Harry Hannin, manager of the Harlem Globetrotters basketball team.

Before Kupcinet was able to make contact with his old friend, he himself received a letter from Hannin. 'You'll never believe this ...' it began.

It transpired that, during a stay at the Hotel Meurice in Paris, Hannin had opened one of the drawers to find a necktie with Kupcinet's name on it.

———➤●◄———

Bunny on the Run

A young girl's favourite toy, apparently on a mission to make a break for it, was thwarted twice in its dramatic attempts to escape. Seven-year-old Lucy Jones carried Bunny, a stuffed rabbit, with her everywhere she went, much to the anxiety of her parents, who knew losing it would be akin to losing a beloved pet or grandparent.

On their way to a skiing holiday in France, Lucy managed to abandon Bunny in the play area of a cross-Channel ferry, and it was only thanks to a kind trucker having seen her with it earlier – and his bravery in spending the rest of the voyage scouring the ship with a girl's toy in his hand – that she ever got him back. But that evening at the ski resort, after Lucy's parents had unpacked the car in driving snow, Bunny was nowhere to be found. The rest of the holiday was a disaster.

The following spring, however, Lucy received a package containing a weathered but nonetheless recognizable Bunny, and a note from the chalet owner in France. It turned out that Bunny had fallen out of the car when the family arrived for their holiday and had spent the whole winter encased in ice on the driveway. When the snow finally melted and revealed the bedraggled rabbit, the woman had remembered the English family with the inconsolable daughter and shipped Bunny back home.

IT IS WRITTEN

It's cheap, ubiquitous and easy to reproduce, and yet the printed word crops up remarkably often in tales of irreplaceable things found.

———⟫●⟪———

GOT YOUR NUMBER

On holiday in Ibiza in 2001, a young woman from Edinburgh met a young man from London and he gave her his number on the back of a bar receipt. But when she got home, the receipt was nowhere to be found.

Chalking it up to carelessness, she called her mother to tell her about the holiday – only for her suitor to answer the phone. She had misdialled her mother's mobile number, which was only one digit different from his.

———⟫●⟪———

After Careful Consideration ...

In 1992, a would-be novelist from Notting Hill completed his manuscript and sent it off to a publisher. Inevitably many months passed before he got her response – and when it came one morning, the verdict was rather more brutal than he had feared.

The pages of his cherished manuscript were lying, wet and crumpled, all over his front garden.

Unable to accept this unorthodox rejection, he phoned the editor and demanded to know what on earth she was thinking, only for her to express incredible relief: she had been hoping all weekend that the manuscript would turn up. Her bag had been stolen from a nearby restaurant on Friday night and the thieves had evidently thrown the 'worthless' bundle of paper over the first garden fence they passed.

From Parrish to Paris

In Paris in the 1920s, American novelist Anne Parrish was idly perusing the shelves of a second-hand bookshop when she came across a children's

classic she had loved as a young girl: *Jack Frost and Other Stories*. Filled with nostalgia she showed it to her husband, Charles, and told him how it had been one of her favourites. Charles opened the book to flick through it and immediately stopped dead: on the flyleaf was written 'Anne Parrish, 209 N. Weber Street, Colorado Springs, Colorado'.

―――――>●<―――――

On the Money

On his way to a date with new girlfriend Esther, Paul Grachan stopped at a sandwich shop in Arlington Heights, Chicago, to buy a snack. As he was paying he noticed that one of his dollar bills had 'ESTHER' scrawled on it, which seemed a funny coincidence so he kept hold of it.

The following week, thinking it would make a cute gift, Paul bought a clear Perspex frame and positioned the dollar bill inside so that it looked as if it was floating. During their next date he proudly presented Esther with what he had christened the Immaculate Dollar of Arlington Heights. She was stunned – considerably more so than Paul had intended.

He asked her what was wrong but all she would say was, 'Don't worry – I'll tell you another time.'

Years later, when they were married and moving into a new apartment, Paul found the Immaculate Dollar at the bottom of a box. He asked Esther if she would finally explain her strange reaction to it.

Esther revealed that, before ever meeting Paul, she had worked as a cashier in a shop. Bored one day, and wondering idly whether she would ever find true love, she had written her name on a dollar bill and told herself that the man who ended up with it would be her future husband. The note had then gone off into circulation and she'd forgotten all about it – until Paul gave it to her as a gift.

'We don't even wear wedding bands,' Esther commented on radio show *This American Life* after fourteen happy years of marriage. 'I mean: why? I know I'm stuck with him.'

———➤●◄———

Signed By the Author

To prepare for his role in the 1974 film adaptation of George Feifer's *The Girl from Petrovka*, the actor Anthony Hopkins scoured London for a copy of the book, but to no avail. Later, as he waited for a train on the platform at Leicester Square, he saw an abandoned book on a bench and was amazed to find it was the very novel he'd been searching for.

But the story doesn't end there. During filming in Vienna, George Feifer visited the cast on set. While talking to Hopkins, he happened to mention that he no longer owned a copy of his own book, since lending the last one to a friend who had misplaced it somewhere in London. Incredulous, Hopkins produced the book he had found by chance – it was the very same copy, complete with Feifer's own annotations in the margins.

———➤●◄———

Megalithic Maths

Colin Wilson, author of a number of books on the occult, has described how he once stumbled across a key piece of information while doing research. He had been reading a book about Stonehenge and other ancient standing stones, in which the author described one particular site as having functioned rather like a Stone Age computer. Wilson made a mental note to find out more about the subject. The next book he picked up was about maths. It fell open in the middle of chapter 6, where he was astonished to see a footnote on the subject Stone Age calculation.

'The chances against coming across it were probably a million to one,' he commented.

———➤●◄———

INCOMING

You've looked under the mattress, behind the fridge and at the back of every drawer. But don't forget to look up!

———➤●◄———

FROM ME TO YOU

At a garden party to celebrate her grandparents' gold wedding anniversary in 2001, ten-year-old Laura Buxton from Staffordshire, England released a helium balloon and watched it float away. She had attached her name and address in the hope that somebody would find her balloon and write back.

Sure enough, she soon received a letter – from a ten-year-old girl named Laura Buxton. This Laura Buxton lived in Wiltshire, 140 miles from Staffordshire.

'I thought it was really weird,' said Wiltshire Laura Buxton, 'because it has come a long way and I am a Laura Buxton too.'

The two girls began exchanging letters and discovered they had even more in common than they thought: both owned a guinea pig and a rabbit, and a three-year-old black Labrador.

EYES ON THE PRIZE

Harry Parr-Davies was an accompanist for Gracie Fields and writer of some of her most famous songs, among them World War II classic 'Wish Me Luck as You Wave Me Goodbye'.

Alas, on a 1939 Atlantic crossing on the *Queen Mary* with Fields, Parr-Davies appeared to run clean out of luck, possibly while waving someone goodbye, when his glasses fell overboard. He was too short-sighted to read music without them, and in some embarrassment went to report his mishap to Fields. She in turn marched to the purser's office to find out if there was any hope of buying a new pair on board – which there was not.

Just at that moment, however, a steward appeared and pinned a notice to the purser's door: 'Found: pair of spectacles. Apply purser.' Inexplicably, or so it seemed, they were Parr-Davies' own glasses.

'Most extraordinary thing,' a passenger from a lower deck later told reporters. 'I opened my porthole and put my hand out to see if it was raining. And into my hand fell a pair of glasses.'

Bombs Away

Many decades after the end of World War II, unexploded mines and bombs continue to be discovered the world over. Mercifully few of them are found mysteriously falling from the sky, but it has been known to happen.

On 7 February 1958, a 1942 artillery shell, branded with the German cross-and-eagles insignia, fell to the ground in Naples, Italy. Then, on 2 January 1984, seventy-nine-year old Fred Simons of Lakewood, California heard a 'resounding crash' and went outside to investigate. There was a four-foot crater in his patio, and at the bottom of it an unexploded twenty-two-pound World War II missile. Even the Federal Aviation Authority had no idea where it had come from.

WE'LL MEET AGAIN

Have you ever had that funny feeling that you've met somebody before? Or completely lost touch with someone only to rediscover them in the most unlikely circumstances? Or encountered a stranger with whom you share a magnetic yet unexplainable connection? You're not the only one …

———⟫●⟪———

'Everything in life is luck.'

DONALD TRUMP

FAMILY FORTUNES

Relatives can be infuriating, meddling, judgemental and downright embarrassing – but, as the saying goes, we can't choose them. They're ours whether we like them or not. But what if we *do* like them but are kept apart by the machinations of fate? Well, more often than not, it seems, fate will conspire to bring us back together again.

———⟶●⟵———

RIGHT BEHIND YOU

Ten years after divorcing his first wife and losing contact with his daughter, Lisa, Michael Dick of east London decided it was time to make amends. Knowing only that she had been taken to Sudbury, Suffolk, by her mother a decade earlier, Mr Dick travelled there and tried to find her in the phone book and electoral records, but to no avail. In desperation he went to the local newspaper, the *Suffolk Free Press*, and they agreed to run a story about his fruitless search. A photographer met Mr Dick in Sudbury and took a picture of him with his two younger daughters to accompany the article.

In a series of remarkable coincidences, Lisa did indeed see the photo while on a visit to her mother from her own home in Essex, and she was astounded – not only to see her long-lost father's face in the paper, but also to spot herself and her mother in the background of the shot.

'I was just completely shocked,' she told reporters after an emotional reunion with her father. 'Me and my mum had been standing in the exact place where the picture was taken about a minute earlier, and you can see us in the picture walking away. It's incredible.'

———➤●◄———

CELEBRITIES REUNITED

The actress Liv Tyler wasn't always Liv Tyler. In fact, according to her birth certificate, Liv began life in 1977 as Liv Rundgren, daughter of the model Bebe Buell and the rocker Todd Rundgren. However, unbeknownst to the infant Liv, her mother had had a relationship with Aerosmith frontman Steven Tyler that had, shall we say, coincided with her relationship with Rundgren, and which had resulted in Liv's conception.

At the age of seven, the young Liv Rundgren met Steven Tyler for the first time and felt an unusual connection to the charismatic star. Two years later, Liv bumped into a girl who looked uncannily like her at an Aerosmith concert. The girl was Mia, Steven Tyler's daughter. Not long thereafter things started fitting into place and Liv confirmed her suspicions that Steven, not Todd, was her true biological father. Three years later, at the tender age of twelve, Liv changed her surname, and the rest is Hollywood history.

———⇒➤●◄⊂———

TWIN TROUBLE

The close connection between twin siblings is well documented. They are reported to feel each other's pain, and profoundly feel the loss of each other if one dies or they are forcibly separated. A 2008 story from the UK captures this close connection in a rather unfortunate way.

Arguing for the right of children to know who their parents are, the MP Lord Alton raised the case of an unnamed couple who married each other only to find out they were twin siblings estranged since birth! The unfortunate pair were thankfully granted a quick, secret annulment in the High Court.

A much nicer story from the same year is that of twin brothers Craig and Mark Sanders and twin sisters Diane and Darlene Nettemeier, who met each other on a double date in Las Vegas and were married in a joint ceremony shortly thereafter. The two families soon built side-by-side homes and then, despite extraordinary odds, Diane and Craig went on to have identical twins of their own.

Oh, Brother

A woman in Gwent who had spent years trying to track down her long-lost brother was amazed when she discovered he lived across the road from her house.

Rose Davies had been raised by foster parents and only later been told she had three brothers. Sid and John had been relatively easy to find but there was no trace of Chris. Little did she know that she had already befriended him and his family.

'I'd only known them for three months,' she commented, 'but I thought they were very nice.'

———⟫●⟪———

Separated at Birth

Shortly before Christmas 1948, a young woman from Northumberland, England gave her baby daughter up for adoption. Poor and unstable, and already struggling to take care of another daughter, Mercia gave little Jenny to an older couple who had been trying for many years to conceive.

Jenny enjoyed her upbringing in Newcastle with the doting adoptive parents she assumed were her own, but just a few miles down the road her sister Helen was suffering abuse and neglect at the hands of her violent stepfather and troubled mother. Neither girl had any idea that the other existed. It was only thanks to a chance outburst by Jenny's cousin during a teenage argument – 'You're not even part of this family; your mam isn't your real mam' – that the story began to unravel.

It was to be a long-drawn-out process, however; as bad luck would have it, Mercia and her husband moved to South Africa with Helen around this time and it was not until the early 1980s that Jenny was able to trace her birth mother to an address back in Northumberland – and not until 2007, three years after Mercia's death, that the sisters finally met.

But the biggest shock was yet to come: after undergoing a DNA test, Jenny and Helen found out they were in fact twins – a shock for Helen, in particular, who aged almost a year and a half thanks to the discovery. Her parents had told her she was born on 4 April 1950, whereas she was of course born on the same day as Jenny: 2 December 1948.

'I went from being sixty-two to being nearly sixty-four in the blink of an eye,' she told the *Guardian* newspaper. 'All my life I'd been reading the wrong horoscope. I thought I was Aries, when in fact I'm Sagittarius!'

———————⇒●⇐———————

FAMILY FATE

It would be fair to assume that 1865 was a difficult year for relations between the families of President Abraham Lincoln and John Wilkes Booth, given the latter's assassination of the former on 12 April 1865. But an unlikely encounter just a few months earlier had promised so much …

One wintry evening in early 1865, a train conductor was selling tickets to a busy crowd on the platform at Jersey City. One of the passengers milling around the train door waiting his turn was twenty-one-year-old Robert Todd Lincoln, son of the president. In the jostle of people he was crushed against the train just as it began moving and fell into the gap between train and platform. A gory tragedy was just seconds away when, in Lincoln's own words, 'my coat collar was vigorously seized and I was quickly pulled up and out to a secure footing on the platform'.

He turned to thank his rescuer and saw that it was a man 'whose face was of course well known to me': internationally acclaimed Shakespearean actor Edwin Booth, the greatest Hamlet of his era, Unionist sympathizer – and elder brother of assassin John Wilkes Booth.

———⇒⊃●⊂⇐———

'Come what may, all bad fortune is to be conquered by endurance.'

VIRGIL

———⇒⊃●⊂⇐———

Don't Know Where, Don't Know When …

The lyrics of Vera Lynn's wartime hit 'We'll Meet Again' were to have an unexpected poignance for Joseph Russell and his sister Nellie. The siblings sang the song together just before Joe was shipped off to the battlefields of Europe – and then they lost touch for more than six decades.

Unbeknownst to Nellie and Joe, they had in fact spent their adult lives living just a couple of miles apart in Greater Manchester, England. Fortunately they were eventually able to make up for lost time when, aged 82 and 79, they wound up in the same nursing home.

'Nellie recognized him immediately and said, "That's my brother",' nursing home manager Pam Capper told reporters. 'It's a moment we'll never forget.'

In an added twist, both siblings had a daughter named Sandra.

<hr>

INSTANT INHERITANCE

An errant gambler and his long-lost son were reunited in the most bizarre circumstances at a poker table in San Francisco in 1858.

Robert Fallon had just won $600 at the table when his fellow gamblers accused him of cheating and shot him dead. Needing to find a substitute to take on the ill-gotten $600 so that they could continue their game, the gamblers invited a young man who happened to be passing to join them.

It was not long before the police arrived to investigate the murder of the man who was presumably still lying in the middle of the saloon, but by this time the newcomer had increased the 'unlucky' $600 to $2,200. The police demanded the $600 that had been in the possession of the deceased before he died, so that they could pass it on to his next of kin – who, as it happened, was the young gambler himself. He had not seen his father for seven years.

<hr />

THE COURSE OF TRUE LOVE …

Love at first sight is all very well, but, as these stories demonstrate, unexpected circumstances often conspire to create an awfully long time between first sight and second sight.

An Apple a Day

Antonin Nowak, a young Polish Jew, spent World War II incarcerated in a Nazi concentration camp. His only joy during this bleak period was the occasional glimpse of a pretty Polish girl on the other side of the fence; sometimes they were able to speak to each other, and she began bringing him apples. She told him her name was Antonina.

In 1944 Antonin was transferred to another prison camp. He was certain he would never see his brave friend again. He survived the war, however, and emigrated to the United States.

Life was better for Antonin but he remained alone, and lonely. In 1957 his friends decided enough was

enough and packed him off on a blind date. The woman, Anita, had also emigrated from Poland after the war and the two of them got to talking about the concentration camps. Antonin spoke of the pretty girl who had brightened his days by bringing him apples, to which Anita had an unexpected response: she was that very girl! She had changed her name after arriving in the States.

Their tearful reminiscences were enough to rekindle an old flame: just hours later, Antonin and Antonina were engaged. They remained together for the rest of their lives.

———⟫●⟪———

BEACH ROMANCE

Reminiscing one day about her magical childhood holidays, Shirley Peskett dusted off her parents' old photo album and flicked through it with her husband, John. One picture in particular, of Shirley building a sandcastle, caught his eye.

'I thought, "That woman there looks just like my mum",' he later told the *Daily Mirror*. He then spotted a football and a bag that looked very much like his own boyhood possessions.

Gradually the story fell into place: despite having grown up on opposite sides of England, both had spent the summer of 1963 on the same Somerset beach with their parents. It wasn't until eleven years later, when they coincidentally ended up at the same Hertfordshire college, that they finally said 'hello' to one another – and, not long after, 'I do'.

<hr />

Ex Marks the Spot

On a holiday in Marrakech, Morocco, a young American couple were enjoying a romantic meal and doing what couples do best: analyzing and maligning their respective exes.

Kate was in mid-flow about a former flame when her boyfriend asked, 'And what did this guy look like?'

'Oh, my God,' she said suddenly, one hand over her mouth and the other pointing across the crowded restaurant. 'He looked just like that.'

As the couple revealed to listeners of radio show *This American Life*, they were indeed sitting just a few steps away from Kate's ex.

LOVE AT FIRST SIGHT

Looking through a family photo album just days before their wedding, Alex and Donna Voutsinas stopped at an astonishing photo of young Alex with his father at Disney World. The astonishing thing was that Alex and his father happened to be in the background; in the foreground were Donna and her siblings, posing with a Disney World character.

'I was glad he proposed before the picture,' Mrs Voutsinas later said, 'because I know that it's because he loves me and not because he thought it was meant to be, it was fate.'

Better Late than Never

George and Jessie first met as teenagers in the late 1950s in London. They were very much in love but neither set of parents approved of the relationship; his family was Christian whereas hers was Jewish. They continued to meet in secret but lost touch when Jessie's parents moved with her to the United States.

Many decades later, after the death of her parents, Jessie found a bundle of unopened letters from George in the attic and realized her mother must have hidden them from her. Now a widow herself, Jessie took the letters with her on a holiday to Spain, thinking she would read them in beautiful, peaceful surroundings. While there she was approached by a man of her sort of age at the hotel bar – who, after a minute or two of polite conversation, introduced himself as George, a recent divorcee.

Suddenly the whole story fell into place for Jessie, who revealed to the astonished man that she was his long-lost girlfriend. They finally married the following year.

MEET THE PARENTS

To celebrate their recent engagement, Stephen Lee and his fiancée Helen organized a dinner party at which his mother and her parents would meet for the first time. After the meal, the parents were so enjoying reminiscing about their childhoods in Korea and their subsequent emigration to the United States

that Stephen took out a photo album to show Helen's family pictures of his late father.

All of a sudden, Helen's mother went pale.

'What did you say his name was?' she asked.

It transpired that, decades ago in Korea, she and Stephen's father had been engaged. The only reason they hadn't married, she revealed, no doubt to awkward looks all round, was that her father didn't approve and had found someone better.

BACK FROM THE DEAD

The notion that the dear departed may have left things unsaid or undone is what leads people to believe in ghosts and spirits. Indeed, as these stories show, those who appear to have passed away can have funny ways of visiting from beyond the grave …

Final Farewell

When Jim Wilson and his sister Muriel heard in 1967 that their father had passed away in Natal, South Africa, they were especially saddened not to have had the chance to see him one last time; Jim lived in England, Muriel in Holland. Muriel's husband was travelling on business and was able to make an immediate detour to South Africa. While changing planes in the Canary Islands he was astonished to find a postcard showing a beach scene in Natal, and he sent it to Muriel in the hope that she would see it as some sort of sign – which she most certainly did: upon close inspection she realized her father was in the photograph, peacefully walking along the seafront.

Slow Progress

In 1960 a tortoise named Chester, the pet of eight-year-old Malcolm Edwards, made a break for freedom and escaped from the family garden. The distraught lad had all but given Chester up for dead when a neighbour announced that she had found him. The slow-moving reptile had wandered an incredible 750 yards through the village of Lyde, Hertfordshire – although what was even more incredible was that thirty-five years had elapsed in the meantime.

'It appears that Chester has been living wild since he escaped from the garden in 1960,' Mr Edwards, by now a father himself, told reporters in 1995. 'I knew immediately I saw him that it was the same tortoise.'

Having brought him back safely to the family home, Mr Edwards added: 'We're hoping Chester might decide to stay this time.'

Holy Hamster

Every pet-sitter's nightmare came true for Gloucestershire couple Lisa Kilbourne-Smith and James Davis on Good Friday 2013 when Tink, the hamster they were watching for friends, shuffled off her mortal coil. After calling the owners to tell them the embarrassing news, Lisa and James gave Tink a respectful send-off in the garden and buried her a foot underground.

Tink was evidently au fait with the Easter story, however, for she staged a miraculous resurrection later that weekend. It emerged that her 'cold and lifeless' state had in fact just been plain old hibernation.

'It's amazing she survived, really,' Lisa's father told reporters after discovering Tink rummaging around in the recycling. 'The energy she had to dig herself out of that hole was remarkable.'

BIBLIOGRAPHY

Hough, Peter, *Phillip Schofield's One in a Million* (Michael O'Mara, 1996)

Plimmer, Martin and Brian King, *Beyond Coincidence* (Icon Books, 2004)

Shircore, Ian, *Conspiracy!* (John Blake, 2012)

Wiseman, Richard, *Quirkology: The Curious Science of Everyday Lives* (Macmillan, 2007)

www.cracked.com

www.snopes.com

www.thisamericanlife.org

www.67notout.com